A ZEBRA IN LION COUNTRY

///////////////////////////////

RALPH WANGER'S
INVESTMENT SURVIVAL GUIDE

RALPH WANGER
President, Acorn Investment Trust

with Everett Mattlin

Simon & Schuster

SIMON & SCHUSTER
Rockefeller Center
1230 Avenue of the Americas
New York, NY 10020

Designed by Irving Perkins Associates

Manufactured in the United States of America

10   9   8   7   6   5   4   3   2   1

Library of Congress Cataloging-in-Publication Data

Wanger, Ralph.
    A zebra in lion country : Ralph Wanger's investment survival guide
/ Ralph Wanger with Everett Mattlin.
      p.   cm.
    Includes index.
    1. Investments.   2. Securities.   3. Finance, Personal.
I. Mattlin, Everett B.   II. Title.
HG4521.W193   1997
332.6—dc21   97-2257
                                                    CIP

ISBN 0-684-82970-3

To Leah,
my partner in life

CONTENTS

PREFACE: A GUIDING HAND WITH A LIGHT TOUCH

Are you standing in a bookstore by the personal finance shelves, trying to decide which book to buy? There they are, the lot of them, in their important-type jackets, all more or less proclaiming Six Infallible Rules That Will Make You a Millionaire.

So how is this book different?

First, it's fallible. When it comes to the stock market, there are no cinches. The stories in this book cover a quarter of a century of my life on the mutual fund battlefield. I've done well enough to survive with honor, but I've made my share of mistakes along the way. Some of the mistakes are recounted herein. I think you learn at least as much from screwups as you do from successes.

Second, there are plenty of ideas in this book. Many books are based on a couple of decent ideas that could be expressed on one sheet of paper but have been blown up into a $24.95 book. I've written a hundred quarterly reports to shareholders of the Acorn Fund and tried to put an original idea in every one of them. You'll find a bunch of those ideas here.

Third, you might have some fun. At least, that's my intention. Stocks go up and down, but humor is forever.

If Ya Done It, It Ain't Braggin'

We've been told often enough that all we need do to retire rich is to start early to save and invest, and favor stocks over bonds or baseball cards.

Good advice. But it does leave a question or two unanswered. Like, "Okay, but which stocks?" And (I can also hear you muttering), "Why should I turn to this guy Wanger for the answer?"

I can understand why you'd ask that. People who do what I do for a living have lost considerable credibility. I'm sure you've read that something like 80 percent of professional managers deserve to be topped with a dunce cap and sent to stand in the corner. They have failed to provide any better results than if their shareholders had passively accepted whatever the market chose to give them—that is, if they had sat quietly in an index fund. Finance theory suggests that in the long run an index fund will indeed beat four out of five actively managed mutual funds. So it is gratifying to be able to state that—at least as of the end of 1996—I am one of the fortunate fifth. The Acorn Fund, which I've been managing since its launch in 1970, has given its shareholders an average annual return (through the third quarter of 1996) of 16.8 percent, while the Standard & Poor's 500 Index has managed 13.1 percent. That kind of differential adds up to big bucks over twenty-five years; we'll look at the numbers later.

You could say I was lucky, and often I have been. But one suspects that something more than luck has been at work. You can be lucky for five years, maybe ten. But twenty-five? Any system successful for that long would seem to have more going for it than just chance.

Also, as you will see, my approach to the market was decided upon right from the fund's beginning. This is a way of investing that has weathered every sort of market.

If I begin with this unseemly boasting, it is only to establish credibility for the philosophy and methods that provided those returns. After all, they are why you are reading these pages.

I don't claim that mine is the only way to confront the market. I invest in small companies with growing earnings whose stocks I still consider good value. I expect that most of my readers also will want exposure to other stocks and strategies. That's fine with me. There are many plausible investment strategies. Any of them can be made to succeed if the practitioner has intelligence and creativity and consistency. But perhaps I can convince you that my approach to the market is one way you, too, should adopt.

Maybe you buy stocks on your own, maybe you invest through mutual funds, maybe you do both. Whatever your way, you are still the one who is ultimately responsible for how your money is invested and what kind of return it brings you. I will explain how I select stocks and when I am likely to sell them, which I hope will be useful to direct investors. But even mutual fund investors have to understand what the managers they hire do with their money. I will try in this book to take you inside one fund's offices and one manager's mind, to give you an idea of how Acorn's merry band goes about its business.

There is little in these pages that is difficult to understand. There are no Greek-letter equations or directions for tearing apart balance sheets. What I will emphasize are the principles, more than the details, of investing. We'll tackle the big-picture questions:

Do you really have to choose between "growth" and "value" stocks or funds?

How reliable is the growth concept, anyway?

How do you get a handle on all those stocks and funds so you can be a real investor instead of a rudderless trader?

Is international investing just a fad?

Is there a time when you should sell your stocks or fund shares and just sit on the sideline for a while?

How do you develop an investment philosophy that promotes patience during the rough spells and the discipline to overcome rash responses to breaking news?

These are crucial issues for all investors, both do-it-yourselfers and fund buyers. How principles are put into daily practice may vary from investor to investor, but it is the overarching approach to the market that in the end is the most important factor in determining investment success. Sharing what I have learned over twenty-five years should contribute to your understanding of what moves markets and individual stocks, and help you decide upon your own investment course.

Don't expect a double-your-money-in-half-the-time book. Your goal should be a steady accumulation of wealth. Lotteries are a fool's game. Indeed, I am highly skeptical of much of what I read and hear daily about market opportunities. History suggests that most of today's hot new stock issues will be in cold storage in five years.

Of course, that doesn't mean you can't try to make 16.8 percent a year instead of 13.1 percent!

The Times That Try Men's Patience

Average annual returns, of course, mask the fact that some years were exceptionally generous and some years frustrating, even bitter. It didn't take me long to find out about the unpleasant stretches.

The Acorn Fund was born on December 31, 1969, "just in time," as I wrote in my first annual letter to my tiny flock of shareholders, "to wish we were in some other business." April and May of 1970 brought one of the "severest bear markets since the 1930s." In just the short time from inception to midyear the value of the infant fund's shares dropped by nearly a third.

Fortunately, the market rallied in the second half of 1970, or we could have been stillborn. And 1971 was robust; we were up 30 percent that year. But the following year we moved into a highly frustrating era. The only stocks moving higher were the big, glamorous, high-visibility companies. The stocks of small, often little-known companies, which have always been Acorn's turf, trailed badly, even though the companies themselves were performing just fine. Then, before small-company stocks had a chance to catch up, the bear market of 1973–74 arrived, and all stocks, mighty and obscure, fell off the cliff. In 1973, Acorn was down 24 percent, and in 1974, another 28 percent.

A recovery followed, but after six years the net asset value of a share of Acorn was only where it had been when we started the fund.

During those maddening years, when contemplating the stony soil in which our Acorn had been planted and trying to retain some shred of perspective and confidence, I could only shake my head and laugh. I decided then, and have reaffirmed often since, that tough markets are no time to be serious. That's when you need the tonic of comic relief.

My first quarterly newsletters to shareholders had been as serious and stuffy as those of other mutual fund managers. I pontificated about monetary and fiscal policy, speculated on the likely direction of the prime rate, and poked about in piles of statistics for clues to the market's mood tomorrow and the day after. It is startling and enlightening to reread some of those first letters and find that the chief concerns of the early 1970s were inflation, the federal deficit, the balance of payments, and high interest rates. If you wait for problems to disappear before investing in stocks, you'll never commit—or earn—a penny.

Faced with a portfolio of perfectly good companies whose stocks were going nowhere, I dropped the usual high-sounding rhetoric about the state of the economy, the market, and the nation and tried to inject some fun into my musings. After all, the gain or loss for any quarter can be stated quickly, and any commentary after that is superfluous. As for market forecasts, they soon go stale. I decided I wouldn't be one of those fund runners who scribbles a page of bland economics followed by "Happy New Year, I'm sorry I lost all your money." If most mutual fund communications are both boring and wrong, well then, I figured, I'd rather be lively and wrong.

So I kept my stock market comment to bikini format. I wanted to cover the essential parts of the subject with a minimum of material. I then moved on to other matters of interest at the time, because there is little that happens in the world that isn't reflected, to some degree, in what prices investors will pay for stocks. And when it's appropriate—and sometimes when it's inappropriate—I prefer the lighter touch.

I decided also early on that I would file away any good quotes I came across in my reading and share them with my investor family at appropriate moments. Often, though, I find I have quotes echoing in my head whose authors I have forgotten. So I follow this rule: if you can't remember who said it, and it's about money, attribute it to John Maynard Keynes, and if it's not, credit Mark Twain.

Deciding to write lively letters turned out to be smart business strategy, though that wasn't my conscious motive at the time. By taking a different tack from my peers and treating the investment business with something less than reverential sobriety, I attracted attention to my scarcely known fund. I then and there concluded that, in this world, if you're too serious, nobody pays any attention to you. However profound and uplifting the essays of Ralph Waldo Emerson, it's perceptive, funny Mark Twain whom people read after high school.

This offbeat approach indeed succeeded in bringing the fund recognition. Newspaper and magazine reporters, weary of summarizing pomposities, have been happy to spice up their columns with some of my sass. The fund's growth is attributable to the columns in another way: some people have written to tell me they became shareholders just so they can receive the reports, which makes the quarterlies the world's most expensive literary magazine.

The Levity Lens

But aside from winning recognition for the fund and keeping up the spirits of suffering shareholders—not to mention my own—humor can perform a very practical role in the investment process. As long, that is, as I keep the jokes in the copy, not in the portfolio.

It has rightly been said that all investors worth their salt must have a contrarian streak in them. If you go with the consensus, your performance will be consensus—ho-hum average. If you want to buy a stock when it is cheap, you have to go against the grain: It is cheap because most people think it should be and will stay cheap until the company is downsized, upgraded, or turned inside out (even though its recent poor earnings could be nothing more than the equivalent of a head cold). And when a stock is skyrocketing, you've got to question the prevailing euphoria relentlessly, too.

Humor helps, for what is humor but a way of pulling back and looking at things from a different angle, seeing the absurdities, challenging the established wisdom, and skewering complacency?

If you take things (including yourself) too seriously, you will probably miss the critically important changes that are occurring around you. Doggedly serious people tend to spend their time justifying the world as it is. They have trouble with the new, because new things are hard to understand and therefore intimidating, even a bit frightening.

In the investment world, the serious, establishment people stick with the so-called blue chips, secure in the belief that what is now respectable can be counted on to behave well forever. Well, it can't. Fifteen years ago Schlumberger was the favorite stock of most institutional investors, and though it is still a major company, its superstar status is long gone. Ten years ago, IBM's dominance of the computer industry was considered unbreakable. For that matter, a hundred years ago the company considered the best managed and most profitable in the country was the Pennsylvania Railroad.

Superior investors, then, look at the current icons with a high degree of skepticism. These folks are the first in the crowd to point out that the emperor is stark naked. And that pretty much defines the role of humor. So much in life is designed to trap you into conformity; the joke and the cartoon help you wriggle free.

For professional investors like myself, a sense of humor is essential for another reason. We are very aware that we are competing not only against the market averages but also against one another. It's an intense rivalry. We are each claiming, "The stocks in my fund today will perform better than what you own in your fund." That implies we think we can predict the future, which is the occupation of charlatans. If you believe that you or anyone else has a system that can predict the future of the stock market, the joke is on you.

I know humor has been invaluable to me as an investor. It clears and sharpens the mind and hones one's contrariness. I highly recommend it. And I hope you accept whatever humor you find in the following pages as more than froth—a lesson in how to look at the investment world afresh.

1

A ZEBRA IN LION COUNTRY

Zebras have the same problems as institutional portfolio managers like myself.

First, both have quite specific, often difficult-to-obtain goals. For portfolio managers, above-average performance; for zebras, fresh grass.

Second, both dislike risk. Portfolio managers can get fired; zebras can get eaten by lions.

Third, both move in herds. They look alike, think alike and stick close together.

If you are a zebra and live in a herd, the key decision you have to make is where to stand in relation to the rest of the herd. When you think that conditions are safe, the outside of the herd is the best, for there the grass is fresh, while those in the middle see only grass that is half-eaten or trampled down. The aggressive zebras, on the outside of the herd, eat much better.

On the other hand—or hoof—there comes a time when lions approach. The outside zebras end up as lion lunch. The skinny zebras in the middle of the pack may eat less well but they are alive.

A portfolio manager for an institution such as a bank trust department, insurance company or mutual fund cannot afford to be an Outside Zebra. For him, the optimal strategy is simple: stay in the center of the herd at all times. As long as he continues to buy the popular stocks, he cannot be faulted. On the other hand, he cannot afford to try for large gains on unfamiliar stocks that would leave him open to criticism if the idea failed.

Needless to say, this Inside Zebra philosophy doesn't appeal to me as a long-term investor.

The above observations were offered to Acorn shareholders some time ago, but I believe them just as valid and vital today, and as relevant to Main Street investors as to Wall Streeters. If you are comfortable only when in the middle of the herd, you might as well sign up for indexing. (Index funds, which track the Standard & Poor's 500 or some other market index, didn't exist back then, but today they're available in mutual fund format.) I'll assume you agree with me that it's worth trying to outrun the pack, because if you were the passive investor sort, you wouldn't be reading this book in the first place.

What triggered the zebra metaphor—and I'm a big believer in the enlightening power of metaphors—was the exasperating investment climate at the time. Some of you have been in the market long enough to remember that at the end of the 1960s and in the first years of the 1970s the market increasingly became two-tiered. The top layer, of "Nifty Fifty" stocks, consisted of a bunch of big, quality, mostly brand-name consumer companies whose stocks were selling at stratospheric price-to-earnings ratios. Disney's P/E climbed to 76, McDonald's to 81, Polaroid's to 97. The second tier—everything else—was selling at more familiar and reasonable P/Es. And since I was then and am now a small-company investor, I was suffering. My *companies* were doing fine, but their *stocks* were trailing badly. I don't think I've ever lived through a more frustrating time in the market.

I held my ground, though: I wasn't going to shed my principles and join the Nifty Fifty nibblers in the middle of the pack. As I quipped to a reporter at the time, "Fundamentally, we still believe that there is only one stock market, not two, and that the market will soon shed a tier."

To an outside observer it probably looked as if professional investors—particularly those in bank trust departments, who managed almost all of the pension money at that time—were manipulating the market, and were in collusion to kite a group of stocks, as in the infamous pools of the 1920s. But it wasn't a conspiracy. It was just the homogeneity of the bank trust departments. Groupthink was pervasive.

It's the same today. Most professional moneymen huddle in the center of the herd. I guess it's to be expected. After all, those responsible for most institutional portfolios have gone to the same colleges and taken the same MBA courses. Once they become money managers at banks, mutual funds, insurance companies, and investment counseling firms, they read the same publications, get fed the same information and opinions on their PCs, talk to the same analysts and institutional salesmen, and attend the same investment conferences, put on by the major brokerage houses. They lunch together, compare notes, and reinforce one another's convictions. They wear the same suspenders or Ferragamo pumps, and switch from Perrier to red wine within the same month. No wonder they end up with nearly identical portfolios, and that the results of those portfolios cluster around the average.

The Nifty Fifty did get their comeuppance, of course. A tier was indeed shed. We had the worst bear market since the 1930s. What I failed to anticipate, though, was that reasonably priced stocks would also drop, as mine did. I learned a lesson that's been repeated many times over the years: when a large segment of the market gets overpriced and eventually corrects, everybody gets nailed. The guilty, the less guilty, and those who are just standing around watching all get into trouble. No matter that you've scorned the high-flyer, crazy-multiple stocks; your sensible portfolio, too, will go down. Your only consolation is that you probably won't be as badly mauled and that your stocks are likely to recover more rapidly, because the former favorites are now on everybody's avoid list.

When a large segment of the market gets overpriced and corrects, *everybody* gets nailed.

Herd on the Street

Herds have a lot of common characteristics, even when the animals are different. Most people can tell a herring from a zebra or a portfolio manager from a sparrow, but their herds act about the same.

Herds are homogeneous. You don't find seagulls in a flock of sparrows, or squid in a school of herring, or insurance salesmen in a herd of portfolio managers. The reason for this last item is interesting. Stockbrokers and portfolio managers both belong to the same human species. Stockbrokers and portfolio managers have systematic differences in personality, however, as measured on a test like Myers-Briggs. (Herring all seem to have the same personality, although they never take the Myers-Briggs test, so it is hard to be sure. It takes years just to teach a herring to hold a pencil.) Portfolio managers tend to be intuition/thinking types (good at objective analysis and ingenious intellectual themes), while salesmen tend to be sensory/feeling types, good at sociability. They consider each other, respectively, eggheads and peddlers, and really don't want to mingle.

Herds have no leaders. Even though gurus such as Elaine Garzarelli or Marty Zweig may trigger a minor stampede, they will not be at the head of the herd for long; their next pronouncement (or their silence) may well be ignored. Sometimes we may suspect that the market is conspiring against us at the behest of some diabolical Dr. No, but there is no such leader, only the reflection of ourselves.

Market herds, like zebra herds, can't run for long without tiring. I never worry if I am early or late with some trend. Rather than chase the herd, we can wait until it comes back by us again.

Some investors were so traumatized by the bear market of 1973–74 they swore off stocks for good. As Mark Twain's Pudd'n-head Wilson once warned, you can get too much out of experience: "The cat that sits down on a hot stove-lid will never sit down on a hot stove-lid again—and that is well. But also she will never sit down on a cold one anymore."

There was so little interest in the market in the mid-to-late seventies that the average daily volume on the New York Stock Exchange fell to 18.6 million shares in 1975 (today, 400-million-share days are considered quiet). Floor traders would pass the time playing pinochle. In five years the average P/E ratio of Nifty Fifty stocks we tracked had fallen from 48 to 13.5. The Inside Zebras had done a complete about-face. Which meant it was a time of extraordinary opportunity for Outside Zebras. When Warren Buffett was asked by *Forbes* in October 1974 how he felt about the market, he replied, "Like an oversexed guy in a whorehouse. This is the time to start investing."

He was right, of course, though a strong upturn didn't arrive until 1982. In August of that year a quiet, dull market was transformed instantly into an enormously powerful bull market on record volume. Why did it happen? Because all portfolio managers wanted to do the same thing at the same time. The herd instinct at work once again.

I didn't know when the market would revive, but I knew it wouldn't stay that cheap forever, so I spent the last half of the seventies gathering bargains. I bought real estate stocks, for example. Herd attitudes were my tip-off. One old friend in the business reminded me that "no institution will ever invest in real estate stocks." Another buddy told me, "Our bank has no real estate stocks on the approved list. We lost too much money in real estate investment trust shares."

I thanked them both sincerely for their advice and immediately bought some Koger Properties and some more Continental Illinois Properties. One sign that the realty stocks were ripe for picking: real estate stocks were then much cheaper than real estate assets. Both American and foreign investors were bidding ten to fourteen times cash flow for quality real estate, while real estate stocks could be bought for five to ten times cash flow. Another signal: the banks' investment people hated the stocks at the same time that their commercial loan departments were loading up on mortgages. Whenever you know that one end of a bank is doing one thing and the other end of the same bank is doing another thing, there's an arbitrage profit potential at hand.

But, you say, real estate eventually took a dive. Yes, but not until eight years later; real estate peaked in 1985. If you can be right for eight years, you're close enough.

Anytime you learn that a group of stocks is despised by an important class of investor—like the largest banks or mutual funds—but you know there are basic values in the group, you can be pretty sure that at some point those people who hate the stocks will come around to adoring them. I'm sure those who advised me to stay away from the real estate stocks were the same persons who took them off my hands a market cycle later. Every few years things change: new people come in, new analysts, and new attitudes.

Look for stocks that have basic value but are out of fashion.

Favor and disfavor in the stock market get overdone time after time. I vividly remember being considered a dangerous loony in the early 1960s, when I was working as a stock analyst, for suggesting to some trust department people that they unload their drug stocks, selling at forty times earnings, and use the money to buy airline stocks, which were dirt cheap. The airlines' transition from propellers to jets lowered costs, so fares came down and demand went up, and for a few years the airline industry was a fast-growth, highly profitable business. In the seventies it was the oil stocks that had a tremendous upsurge, and then they suffered a tremendous decay all through the eighties. These moves can go on for a long time.

In the spring of 1996 technology stocks had enjoyed a huge run, and I began to believe it was time for a breather. The apparel business, on the other hand, had been awful. Wasn't it logical that at some point some woman somewhere would want a new dress? I thought it about time to sell the techs and buy the retailers, and sure enough, in the summer the former took a considerable hit and the retailers started a nice move up.

So Much for Sophistication

Herd instincts are as prevalent as ever. We're all supposed to be more sophisticated investors now, but human psychology doesn't change. In fact, in this day of high-speed telecommunications, money managers quickly react—and overreact—to recent events with frightening unanimity. Long-term thinking has practically disappeared. Institutions stampede into energy or biotechnology or emerging-market stocks and then stampede out again. Charged up by analysts' optimistic earnings projections, they drive a stock to silly heights, only to rush for the exit when earnings come in even a penny or two below the forecast.

With this kind of skittish institutional activity accounting for such a large percentage of the trading, markets have the potential for greater volatility. Market action can be more herdlike than it was when trading was dominated by thousands and thousands of individuals who woke up in the morning with other things on their minds than what stocks they should buy or sell that day. One might think that a small number of well-trained professionals would value securities quite rationally, so that prices would stay close to equilibrium values at all times and markets would be stable. After all, if you were a passenger in an airplane that frequently changed its course and altitude, then rode in a second plane that cruised along in a steady path, wouldn't you feel that the first pilot was a trainee and the second a pro? For that matter, how did we talk you back into the air for a second flight?

Most portfolio managers are intelligent, careful people who have studied their craft about as long as an airline pilot has; but in a world of instantaneous communication, when all of us hear the same news within seconds, our minds seem to leave our gray-suited bodies and well-appointed offices, and we act just like a herd of zebras who have sensed a pride of lions sneaking up on us. Wham! Off we go in an instant.

We really must be grateful that this herd mentality persists, because if it weren't for these overreactions throwing good stocks on the bargain table, it would be a lot harder for the rest of us to make money.

The lesson to be drawn—trite maybe, but as powerful as ever and just as hard to heed—is to buy stocks when nobody wants them. Buying the ones that are out of favor and selling the ones that are most popular—which isn't a bad definition of value investing—does seem to work over a long period of time. Of course, doing it well will give you better results than doing it badly. And something can be despised because it's despicable. You must have confidence that the value is there.

If you want to stand out from the pack, you have to stand outside the pack.

It's easier, I realize, to advise contrarianism than it is to practice it. It takes a strong will to keep from being drawn into the middle of the herd. It's so much more comfortable to play it safe and be an Inside Zebra. But if you want to stand out from the pack, you have to stand outside the pack.

Yes, you may be exposing yourself to more risk, but you can't make money in the market without taking on risk. And there are ways, which we'll consider as we go along, to keep the lions at bay.

2

$\blacktriangledown\!/\!\blacktriangleright$

THINK SMALL

In my first faltering steps down my career path, I landed a job with a firm that was a predecessor of the present-day Harris Associates, at that time a small Chicago brokerage house that also looked after some of its clients' portfolios. I knew a bit about stocks and bonds; I had, as Oscar Levant once put it, a smattering of ignorance. But Irving Harris, whose firm it was, took me under his wing, trained me as a security analyst, and eventually turned me into a portfolio manager.

My first analytic assignment was to go see a company called H. M. Harper, located in a Chicago suburb. It made nuts and bolts, literally—stainless steel nuts and bolts. I had worked in a machine shop for a time, so I knew a turret lathe when I saw one and felt reasonably comfortable when one of the firm's managers took me into the shop. My surprise came when he led me into a second building, which housed a brand-new machine (one the company had been working on for a couple of years) that could make stainless steel extrusions. Stainless steel is extremely difficult to extrude, but the company had finally created a machine that could turn out various structural shapes; the first orders were coming from the aircraft industry. Development of this fancy new tool had cost Harper about $2 million, which had been hurting its profitability, but the machine was ready to roll and the manager assured me the company would be shipping product within days.

I turned to my guide and said, "Let me get this straight. So far this has been a cost, you've had no revenue, right?"

"Right."

"And next week you'll start having revenues, right?"

"Sure."

"And that means your profits will go up a lot, right?"

"Well, yeah, you're right."

Even as a novice, I figured this one out. I went back and told Irving and we loaded up on the stock. Which promptly tripled. I was hooked. I knew the stock market was where I wanted to be.

Ask the Owners

Irving always preferred small companies like H. M. Harper over the General Motors and Exxons and AT&Ts of the world. He was an entrepreneur himself, with several business interests, and he could relate to the entrepreneurial spirit in others. When you look at small companies, you typically find one man or a couple of men (back then, when Irving was breaking me in, they were always males) who work day and night and weekends, forget about vacations, and probably have miserable home lives, because all they really care about is making their vision come true. They own a large enough chunk of stock that their personal interests are right in tune with those of the company's outside shareholders. Irving could sit down with those people, who make all the major decisions for their companies, and see the possibilities they saw; their enthusiasm could become his own.

And Irving's enthusiasm for small companies became mine as well. Researching a big corporation just isn't the same. You usually end up talking to the investor relations officer, but even if you can get to some higher officials, you never know for sure who really makes the key decisions—them or an executive committee or a half-dozen division heads. And you rarely come away with the same sense of excitement. Paid hands, even with the prospect of a bonus, are not the same as the founders and drivers of small companies. At big companies you talk to executives. At small companies you talk to owners. An executive may be good at running a going concern, but it's the owner who is the risk taker able to conceive and create something that can make him and those who invest in him rich.

Just as important, a small company has just one or two businesses, so you can understand it. Big companies, with multiple divisions and broad product lines, are too complex to grasp thoroughly, no matter how much time you spend on them. I remember that many years ago I was surprised that Westinghouse had lost money on a manufactured-housing subsidiary I didn't even know it owned. These days a tobacco company owns a food company, a steel company owns an oil company, an electric turbine manufacturer owns a television network. When a company develops into a multi-industry giant, even the company's top management can't understand all that it does.

At big companies you talk to executives. At small companies you talk to owners.

At this point, you are probably wondering what size company is "small." Any company with a market capitalization of under $1 billion generally qualifies as small-cap these days. (The market capitalization is simply the number you come up with when you multiply the number of shares outstanding by the current price per share.) The market capitalization of General Electric, for purposes of comparison, is about $125 billion.

Small Pays Off Big

But the main reason for preferring small companies is not ease of comprehension or accessibility. I just happen to like the fact that you can make more money with them. You don't have to take my word for that. There are professors who analyze such claims. The most recent study, conducted by Ibbotson Associates, considered stock returns from 1925 through 1995. (There isn't much in the way of reliable stock market data before 1925, but seventy years is a pretty healthy stretch of time.) It found that big companies returned 10.5 percent a year on average, while small companies gave the investor 12.5 percent. Over time, a two-percentage-point advantage makes a huge difference in returns. Even over twenty years, a not unlikely time horizon for investors, $10,000 compounding at the higher rate turns into $105,451, a hefty 40 percent more than the $73,662 that the 10.5-percenter collects. And 10.5 and 12.5 percent are average returns. Doing better than average can create an enormous difference in the outcome.

In recent years, thanks to the extraordinary bull market of the 1980s and 1990s, stocks have been performing well above their seventy-year average. As recorded in the preface, since the Acorn Fund was started in 1970, large-company stocks (as measured by the Standard & Poor's 500 Index) have averaged 13.1 percent a year. Acorn, as also noted, has provided 16.8 percent. The difference in results, after compounding has done its magic, is eye-opening.

VALUE OF $10,000 COMPOUNDING AT 13.1 PERCENT
AND 16.8 PERCENT

	13.1 PERCENT (S&P 500)	16.8 PERCENT (ACORN FUND)
Beginning	$10,000	$10,000
5 years	18,506	21,738
10 years	34,247	47,253
15 years	63,378	102,717
20 years	117,288	223,284
26 years (6/70–6/96)	217,053	485,368

The academics aren't sure why the small-company stocks that are Acorn's territory have done better than large-company stocks. I've asked a half-dozen people who have written PhD theses on the subject to summarize their explanations, and all I get is "Aahhh . . . er . . . hmmmmm . . ." and eventually "I don't know."

A big problem in coming up with an answer is that there are two kinds of small companies. There are the young, possibly rapidly growing companies that are small because they haven't been around long enough to get big. And then there are the other kind, the distressed companies, the formerly big outfits that are losing money, so their stock price and market capitalization have shrunk in tandem. They have had smallness thrust upon them. The day before it entered bankruptcy, Penn Central was a small-cap company.

The academics looking at the returns of small companies want to consider the risk people take to invest in them, and the risks in the two kinds of small companies can obviously be very different. Some of the studies going on now are trying to separate out the two categories.

So the question of "why" is still open; the experts disagree. But we can all understand that some small companies will become successful big companies in a few years, and that they make highly rewarding investments.

Darwinism in the Marketplace

I have a sort of ecological theory to explain the phenomenon of the higher return of small companies. In any environment, some creatures are going to be more successful at adapting than others, and those are the ones that will thrive and prosper. In a tough, competitive business environment, new companies struggle to survive by finding and exploiting their own special niche. Most fail, but the few that make it win big. The reason they make it is that the environment at the time is right for their growth. This can be called a circular argument—if the company grows, then the environment must be favorable—but it is a useful way to think about what causes success or failure.

As an important instance, we had an enormous change in the physical structure of the United States in the 1950s and 1960s, when our vast interstate highway system was built. (Highway construction has been sporadic since.) Entire new sections of the country were opened up for housing, as well as commercial and industrial development. Some people benefited immediately. The dairy farmer became an instant millionaire when his property was needed for a highway interchange. It was dumb luck, the most reliable way to make money.

The highways suburbanized the country; people abandoned city apartments for single-family housing. Everybody then needed at least one automobile, and probably more than one. Drive-in fast-food places sprang up on every corner where there wasn't already a gas station. And the shopping mall was born. Ten years after the malls came, Sears, Roebuck became the number one retail company in the country, and stayed that way for a long time, because it understood the trend and anchored countless malls. (Woolworth, on the other hand, didn't get it. It stayed with its small urban stores too long and never adapted.) Often, the big growth stocks reached their heights because they were boosted by some particular development at the time.

A classic example of the impact of ecology is the growth and decline of IBM. In the 1950s IBM was an important but struggling company, with a good punch-card business and a good typewriter business. Then the computer came along. Why IBM took over that market, and Burroughs, General Electric, Univac, RCA, Honeywell, and Control Data ended up losers, is a complicated story, but the main element, I believe, was IBM's marketing strategy. Its hardware was generally satisfactory, but not great; its marketing, however, was tremendous. It sold its mainframes because it controlled the executive suites of the country. Time after time I heard stories about corporate computer departments recommending a Honeywell or Burroughs computer, but when the purchase order reached the president's desk, he crossed out "Burroughs" and wrote in "IBM." It wasn't because he thought IBM had a better computer for the money, but he liked and trusted the IBM salesman. That, of course, generated profits for IBM that it could then put back into new equipment and programs, until it dominated the market, the way NCR had done before it and Microsoft did after it.

It seemed as if IBM had an unbreakable hold on the computer market—until there was a dramatic shift in the ecology. In the same way that a huge meteorite hit the earth and changed the climate and wiped out the dinosaurs, the invention of the personal computer broke IBM's domination. The dinosaurs couldn't adapt. IBM tried to adapt but was late about it. When it finally got around to making a PC, the product was sufficiently competitive, but IBM's big advantage—control of the purchasing decision—had disappeared.

By that time the buy decision at companies had been pushed down to a different level, because the purchase involved a $2,000 machine instead of a $5 million machine. Department heads are perfectly competent to decide where to spend $10,000 on hardware. Who cares? The marketing decision no longer went up to the president's desk. IBM's selling power was suddenly cut off; the company had suffered a marketing aneurysm. Deals now had to be made with the wrong person (from IBM's point of view), because a good many of the people lower down the line hated IBM. In its glory days, IBM reps had become rather arrogant, knowing they were going up to see the president. They had barely tolerated the humble vice president in charge of computers. But suddenly that VP was the person with the purchasing power, and he was delighted to screw IBM.

Gradually IBM realized what was happening, but it couldn't figure out what to do about it. That happens often when the environment shifts. What happened to IBM was really the same thing that happened to the Pennsylvania Railroad. When the highway system was built, suddenly trucks were the way to move goods, and railroads weren't. Some of the railroads started truck lines. But they required a kind of entrepreneurial spirit that was uncommon among railroad people. The railroad business was so regulated that it was run by a bunch of bureaucrats who spent their days shuffling papers for the Interstate Commerce Commission. There was no way they could rise to the challenge of the highways and build successful trucking companies.*

Ecological changes create great opportunities for the investors who understand them. We'll come back to this concept in a later chapter, on identifying investment themes. Investors also have to watch out for the companies that can't adapt to change, and in today's business world changes come at a dizzyingly rapid rate. If you don't believe it, look back at the favorite growth stocks of yesteryear. You'll find some real giggles on the list and more than a few head scratchers. In the 1960s Polaroid, Burroughs, and Xerox were considered invincible. Later, as recounted, Schlumberger and IBM took on the mantle, and for a good many years Sears was a master of the universe.

The managers of small companies are generally better at re-

---

*Some railroads tried to enter other transportation businesses. The Denver Rio Grande and Western Railroad ran a bus line from 1927 to 1948, when it was sold to Continental Bus System. The bus line was not profitable for Denver Rio Grande, and the sale price, $562,000, wasn't much above book value.

sponding to change. They have the aggressive spirit that's needed. In big companies decisions have to go through layers of management, and things happen slowly. Indeed, in my book, establishment companies are automatically suspect. Twenty years of substantial corporate growth can be a warning sign. Chances are, things have changed enough so that whatever made the company a success twenty years ago doesn't work anymore. Dumbo could fly because he was a baby elephant. Adult elephants are aerodynamically unsound.

Dumbo could fly because he was a baby elephant. Adult elephants are aerodynamically unsound.

By concentrating on smaller companies, then, you improve your chances of catching the next wave and riding with the tide. Look at the corporate crusade of the past five years: downsizing. The big companies decided that to be efficient and competitive they had to decentralize, regionalize, become a flock of small elephants flying in formation. So a small company is the right size now.

More Room to Grow

Obviously, but importantly, small companies can run faster than mature ones. Ford can't sell twice as many cars this year as it did last year, but a small software company can more than double its sales of a hot new program. I've seen the stock prices of small energy companies shoot up overnight when they announced a new gas discovery that wouldn't have created a quiver in Exxon's stock price. Some small companies run fast enough that they pretty quickly graduate into the big leagues and prove enormously rewarding to investors who don't sell them too soon.

You might think that if a company has found its niche and seems to have a clear field ahead of it, word would get around and the price of the stock would reflect it. But that's the beauty of small companies. If you call on big companies, you'll be standing in line. There must be three dozen Wall Street analysts knocking on Microsoft's door every week, and Microsoft sends out reams of data and opinion to institutional investors like myself. So much information is disseminated so quickly, by fax, modem, and conference calls, that it's hard for anyone to get an edge on other investors. Furthermore, the institutional managers react to any news pronto, so developments get reflected in stock prices immediately. That's what the academics mean when they say the market is "efficient."

> Small companies aren't blanketed by research coverage. You can actually discover things that others don't know.

Certainly when you look at the three hundred largest corporations that are followed by platoons of security analysts, you are unlikely to learn anything that other people don't know. You might as well throw the proverbial darts at the proverbial list of blue chips and cross your fingers. But small companies aren't blanketed by that kind of coverage. There aren't enough analysts to follow all of them. You can actually discover things that others don't know.

But When's the Payoff?

Perhaps I have raised a question in your minds: Since small companies don't get analysts' attention, won't they just stay ignored? Why own a cheap stock if it's going to stay cheap?

There are four different ways that a stock price can rise:

1. Growth: As the company grows, the market price of the stock will go up in line with earnings, dividends, and book value. This is generally true even if the company is sparsely followed.

2. Acquisition: The company can be acquired by a larger company at a price well above the market.

3. Repurchase: If a stock sells well below its economic value, the company may repurchase sizable blocks of its own shares.

4. Revaluation: As a company grows and prospers, it can cross the threshold of institutional interest. The ugly duckling is pronounced a swan, and its price-to-earnings ratio increases.

Good-quality smaller companies can produce stock market profits by any of these four mechanisms. The best hope for established, big-company favorites is the first—only one out of four. Large companies have so many shares outstanding that buyback programs seldom have a meaningful impact. And though in recent years we've seen giant companies swallowed by other giants, small companies are obviously more likely targets—and the buyer almost invariably pays well above the market price in order to rake in the shares. Some of my best gains over the years have come from these takeovers.

In our experience, there is no reason to worry about nonrecognition: the sound economic values of good small companies get reflected in their stock prices sooner or later.

A Tale of Two Strategies

Several years ago one of my relatives, recently widowed, asked for my advice. She expected to live on the income thrown off by the investments that she and her husband had made over the years. Should she, then, put nearly all of her money into tax-exempt municipal bonds? It's certainly a course many retired and older people take.

I advised her against it. Inflation always worries me. She was sixty-one years old and could easily live another twenty years, and inflation of even 3 percent over two decades would cut the purchasing power of her dollars nearly in half, which would mean a gradual falloff in her standard of living. Stocks have a better chance of protecting long-term purchasing power: companies can raise prices, earn more money, increase their dividends. But stocks bring market risk, which worried her. So I made up a little story to help make my point.

Once upon a time, two rich men lived in the town of N——, near the mouth of a great river. They both had pondered long on the best way of protecting their gold and silver and carpets and tapestries. In the end, Mr. C built himself a solid stone house and locked his treasures safely in the cellar. Mr. B felt it was better to outrun thieves, who could besiege a house, so he bought a sturdy ship and put his valuables in the hold.

As chanced to happen, next year there was a flood. Mr. B's yacht floated easily enough, but Mr. C's house was inundated and his beautiful possessions ruined by the muddy water. Mr. B sailed up and removed the disconsolate Mr. C from the roof of his nearly submerged house. "You see," said Mr. B, "that flexibility is better than solidity." Mr. C tried to smile at his rescuer.

A few months later Mr. C was back in his bedraggled house. Suddenly, a great storm arose, and tremendous waves threatened to swamp Mr. B's heavily laden boat. In panic, Mr. B threw his fine goods overboard to lighten his ship. This enabled him to steer toward the light from Mr. C's window, drop anchor, and swim ashore to Mr. C's beach. As Mr. C brought poor Mr. B, soaked and forlorn, into his house, Mr. C couldn't help but remark, "There are times when a solid foundation is better than flexibility."

A bond portfolio produces solid income, safe as a stone house, but the floodwaters of inflation will eventually ruin its purchasing power. A stock portfolio has the ability to rise with inflation, but the storms of recession can cause rough sailing and eroded values, at least temporarily.

My advice to the widow was twofold. First, diversify, using an equity portfolio as well as the tax-exempt bonds that generate current income. Second, look for equities that are likely to provide an increasing dividend stream over time. Small but growing companies are an excellent place to start such a search.

Smaller Companies, Bigger Risks

Yes, small companies are riskier. Small companies often stumble trying to become big companies. When you are dependent on one or two people and one or two products, it is easy to see how things can go wrong. One man tries to do too much as his business expands. Another gets ahead of himself. I think of one entrepreneur who would have been a great success with $5 million in capital, but his investment banker raised $100 million and he went berserk, spent the money on unsound expansion, and wound up on the rocks. He never had a chance to grow and learn.

Small is always vulnerable. It's easier to sink a tugboat than a battleship. Not that big companies are sure protection either: IBM is the prime example of the past decade. At one point its stock was in such a free fall that I was waiting for IBM to become a small-cap stock. Trouble lurks everywhere.

But you can't make any money without taking risks. Usually, the greater the risk, the greater the opportunity. Which only seems just: the daring deserve a chance at a bigger prize. The greater-risk-is-needed-to-bring-greater-reward theory has been verified in university laboratories. The so-called Capital Asset Pricing Model that has dominated academic theory about stock prices states that you can earn above-market returns only if you assume greater-than-market risk. Two portfolios of equal riskiness would be expected to bring the same returns.

But there is one major exception (the professors prefer the word "anomaly"). Rolf Banz, a professor at the University of Chicago who has published a number of papers examining the behavior of small-company stock prices, has found that companies with the smallest market capitalization have provided a better-than-average return not only in terms of higher absolute percentage gains but *even after adjusting for their greater risk.*

Big companies have returned 10.5 percent a year, on average, while small companies have returned 12.5 percent. Moreover, small companies outperform large companies *even after adjusting for their greater risk.*

Still, if you gather small-caps, you're always going to have some bad ones in your basket. I've certainly had my share of stocks that kissed the buzz saw. I think with particular pain of Coleco, which fell from 65 to 12 when it introduced a computer that bombed.

Then there was Energy Reserves, whose key drilling prospect in Wyoming turned out to be a dry hole, promptly sinking its stock from 36 to 6. And when the CAT scanner market was decimated by regulatory changes that forced hospitals to cut their budgets, Elscint's stock went from 28 to 8 in short order. Of course, I hadn't bought them at the top. Every debacle of this sort was preceded by a long period of rising prices and euphoria. (This happy period deserves a name of its own. If a collapse is a *de*bacle, can we call the prior rise a "bacle"?)

If you don't make some misjudgments, you're doing it wrong: you've not taken enough risk and you'll never score a big one. You do best when your investments are controversial—when you stray farthest from the herd.

Aside from the risk of the out-and-out failure of companies, small-cap stocks are more volatile, which is another way to look at risk. When a company has only one or two products, its earnings can swing more violently than those of a Procter & Gamble, with thousands of products whose fortunes can offset one another. As a fairly recent concrete example of what volatility means in the real world, the net asset value of Acorn's shares dropped 23.3 percent in just one quarter—the third quarter of 1990 (the market as a whole was down about 15 percent). The investor has to have the stomach for these air pockets.

And even if you can stand the downdrafts, you shouldn't be in the riskier end of the stock spectrum with money you're going to need soon—say, to meet a college tuition payment in the next two or three years. The market gets slammed to the floor with regularity, and it may not struggle up again for a couple of years. And since investors taking their first tentative steps back into a bloodied market generally feel safer with blue chip stocks, it usually takes small-caps longer to regain their footing.

Taking Precautions

There are ways, however, to lower the riskiness of small-caps. You can be very picky about what you buy. For one thing, small is good, micro is not. Often, the smaller the stock, the bigger the risk. For the littlest companies, it's like auditioning for a chorus line: one misstep and you're out. I've made it a practice to stay away from the start-ups, the tiny techs, the near-venture-capital situations. I want companies that are established and whose managements have proven, at least thus far, that they know how to run a company.

> Small is good, micro is not. For the littlest companies, it's like auditioning for a chorus line: one misstep and you're out.

I also stay away from marginal, underfinanced companies of any size, despite whatever speculative potential there may be. I insist on financial strength, which excludes most newly minted companies and turnaround situations. Small companies are proverbially squeezed for working capital, so a sound balance sheet is an important factor in sustaining growth.

> Look for a company that has carved out a special niche for itself.

I'm always looking for a company with a strong position in its industry, which lowers the risk quotient. A small company is frequently able to carve out a special niche for itself and do much better than its competitors. That niche can be geographical, like that enjoyed by a regional bank, utility, or railroad. It can be technological, based on patents and know-how. Sometimes the niche is sim-

Corporate Growth, Nature's Way

Most investors, whether they are interested primarily in large companies or in small ones, focus on growth. They want the ones that are getting bigger and, presumably, more profitable. The idea of economic growth we fixate on, however, is only about two centuries old. Nature has been working on problems of growth, differentiation, and survival for more than 600 million years, a period more than long enough for living creatures to try every growth strategy. It seems reasonable to assume that biology might provide an array of growth strategies that would be powerful metaphors for changes that take place in the structures of corporations.

Let us consider an ambitious young cell of 600 million years ago. She has just gotten her MBA (Model for Biological Activity) and wishes to experience personal growth. She has four basic strategies, all of which have worked well in nature. We will look at them and at analogous corporate strategies, using a hamburger stand, Harry's Hamburger Heaven, as an example.

Expansion. The first method is to simply expand as a single cell. Simplicity is an advantage, for no new structural form must be invented. The disadvantage is that cell life depends on nutrient transfer through the cell wall, and a growing cell doesn't expand its surface as fast as its volume, which mandates the maximum possible size for a single cell.

In our analogy, Harry's Hamburger Heaven can expand a single store for a while, but the size of a single store will be limited by the number of potential customers in its trading area.

Fission. A more efficient growth strategy that has served bacteria well to this day, fission divides the cell into two identical but separate daughter cells. The advantage of fission is conservatism, for the two cells have the same size and structure as their predecessor. The disadvantage is that the cells must remain simple in function and microscopic in size.

Our hamburger stand can model fission by opening a second store as a separate corporation and letting each run its own show.

Chaining. A third strategy is that of the seaweed and the sponge. Cells divide into a mass of identical daughter cells, but instead of separating, the cell walls stick together, forming a chain. This has the advantage of allowing macroscopic size, which opens up some new habitats. The disadvantage is that the chain cannot do very much more than the single cell could.

If Harry's Hamburger Heaven opens forty identical hamburger stands, it would be using a chaining strategy.

Differentiation. The fourth and last strategy is much more complex. Most multicellular organisms, including us, are made up of cells that have taken up different shapes and functions, allowing the development of leaves, stems, bones, fins, eyes, and all the myriad beautiful tissues and organs that are found in the bodies of modern plants and animals. The advantage here, of course, is the ability to evolve and fill every ecological niche. In return for complexity, differentiated cells must accept risk. Very few species of large animals exist for more than 10 million years, while the conservative amoeba is unchanging and therefore immortal.

Most publicly held corporations fit this fourth, dynamic class. Our hamburger joint is now the Fast Food Division of HHH Enterprises, complete with all the possibilities of growth, development, and success or failure inherent in a complex organism.

The four strategies, which work so well in nature, have proved a handy way for our analysts to classify corporate growth strategies. It helps them judge companies' progress and remaining potential. Corporations, too, are living organisms.

ply a marketing technique, the ability to sell a product or service a little bit better than its rivals. What I don't want are me-too companies that rank fifth or sixth in their industry, because their profit margins will rarely be as good as those of the industry leaders.

Several Baskets

To sum up, I believe in investing in quality small companies, seasoned rather than nearly new, with financial strength, dominance in their market segment, entrepreneurial management, and understandability. There are thousands of small companies, but not many that meet these criteria.

But no matter how selective you are, things still go wrong.

Disappointments go with the small-cap territory. That is why diversification is so important. Maybe you've heard about a great little company that seems to have everything going for it, but if that is to be your only small-cap holding, keep your money in the bank. You should own at least a dozen stocks if they are all small-cap, so a couple of winners can offset a couple of duds. A portfolio of well-researched small companies should be no riskier than a portfolio of large, well-known companies. (The need for diversification is also a strong argument for investing in small-caps through mutual funds, which are required by law to be diversified. More on this later.)

A portfolio of well-researched small companies should be no riskier than a portfolio of large, well-known companies.

You need to diversify in another way, also. Your total investment portfolio should include large-company stocks, or large-company mutual funds, along with the smaller fry. For reasons no one has satisfactorily explained, small-cap stocks go through cycles of investor favor. When people comment on the health of "the market," they mean the Dow Jones Industrials or the S&P 500 Index. The chart of the patient in the next bed—that is, small stocks—may look quite different. There are really two distinct markets, and their fortunes alternate.

If we look at recent history, for example, we find that from 1963 to 1968 small-company stocks did better than the blue chips. From 1969 to 1974 it was the blues' turn. From the end of 1974 until mid-1988—a generous, wonderful, eight-and-a-half-year cycle—

the small-caps triumphed. From mid-1983 to the end of 1990, a seven-year stretch, the big-caps won. In the first years of this decade, my kind of stocks gained the ascendancy; then the big boys took over again, in 1994. We have seen some lean years of late, so perhaps we have some fat ones owed us.

> Trying to sell an illiquid stock in a down market brings to mind the galley slaves in *Ben-Hur*, chained to their bench while the ship sinks.

Sure, you can pick small-cap stocks that do well no matter what style's in vogue, but it's harder when you have to swim against the tide. And you are more likely to be faithful to a fickle market if you are getting satisfaction from some part of your portfolio at all times. Style diversification, too, is smart policy.

> There's one sure antidote to the liquidity problem: buy stocks you don't have to sell for a good long time.

There is one other risk in small-caps: trading is difficult. They tend to be illiquid, at least for an institutional manager like myself who owns several thousand shares rather than a couple of hundred. When you want to sell, you find there aren't enough buyers unless you keep knocking down the price you'll accept, and sometimes it seems there are no buyers at any price. I remember—though I'd rather forget it—one stock I tried to unload for two years and never got a bid on any of it. A stock like that just slides from 4 to 3 to 1 and finally disappears altogether, and there's nothing you can do about it. It doesn't kill you as long as you don't do it too often, like a lot of other things. But at times I am reminded of the galley slaves in *Ben-Hur,* who are chained to their seats while the ship is sinking.

There's one sure antidote to the liquidity problem: buy stocks you believe you'll hold on to for a good long time. And I mean years, by which time, if all's gone as hoped, the company will be bigger, many more analysts and investors will be interested in it, and liquidity will be far less of a worry. More important, you'll still have a hefty profit to comfort you if you have to sacrifice a bit of your gain to get out of a position.

3

GROWTH, VALUE, OR GARP?

Gilbert and Sullivan marveled that every boy and girl "that's born into the world alive / Is either a little Liberal / Or else a little Conservative." Reading today's financial press, you'd think that every investor is likewise genetically predestined to enroll in either the growth or the value school of investing.

The growth investor, in case you are at all fuzzy on these matters, is the one who wants companies with earnings growing at least twice as fast as those of most companies—15 percent annually would do nicely, 20 percent even better. If a company's been able to do that for a bunch of years, you feel kind of warm toward it, so you don't mind paying a premium for the stock. How much of a premium depends on how rosy the future looks. If you can see five years more of galloping growth, you are inclined to be especially generous. High P/Es don't upset the growth buyer if the future looks bright enough. If all checks out, he buys the stock and hopes his projections pan out. To belabor a point, the Nifty Fifty crew of the early seventies were exemplars of this species.

The value investor, on the other hand, hates high P/Es, so he won't touch the lionized growth stocks. He's a cheapskate, looking for remnants other investors have discarded but that he thinks are really worth a lot more. His daily hope is to find somebody who has something worth $20 who will sell it to him for $10. His passion is to identify a "value gap" between what he thinks a stock is worth and the price the market currently has pinned on it.

Value investing is a three-step process:

STEP 1: Measure the value of a company and show that its value is higher than its market price, so that a value gap truly exists. Three common value measures are:

Price to book value
Price to cash flow
Private market value, which is roughly what the company would fetch if it were auctioned off tomorrow

STEP 2: Hypothesize an "exit strategy," a way in which the market will come to its senses and push up the market price of the stock to its true value, now known only to you. Some exit strategies:

Company is acquired.
An unprofitable division is sold, so earnings go up.
Other investors see the light, and market upgrades it to a growth multiple.

STEP 3: Buy the stock and wait for the value gap to close.

For the growth advocate, the value of the company's assets isn't meaningful. The important assets for him, such as brands, management skills, patents, or a natural monopoly, don't appear on the balance sheet anyway.

Value investing is basically based on a static analysis, a concentration on value right now. Your value investor might wear a T-shirt that proclaims, "We don't pay for the future." The growth investor thinks about where the company will be in five years.

The market overreacts to news, good or bad.

The growthie buys on good news, such as the approval of a new drug, completion of an R&D project, or the receipt of a big contract. And he sells on bad news: the exit of a key manager, loss of market share, or a negative earnings surprise. It is precisely such events that may whet the value buyer's appetite, for the market tends to overreact to bad news, creating a value gap.

The growth investor is buying what everybody agrees is a great company. The value investor is looking at companies most investors believe are in trouble, which explains their knocked-down price.

The value investor is hitting for singles. He will be delighted if he doubles his money in a couple of years; few value ideas pay off better than that. If his analysis is correct and the company is worth more than the market recognizes, however, the downside is limited. The growth investor is going for home runs. He dreams of making five or even ten times his investment. And his downside is considerable, since high-multiple stocks can become average-multiple stocks at the drop of a penny in expected earnings. You never know for sure if a company's going to do what you hope it will.

A growth stock that works—that delivers 15 percent or more annual earnings growth for five years—will more than double your money. You will also experience the thrill of concluding that you are a financial wizard. The high you get from finding a growth winner is very much like what a poker player feels after taking in four large pots in a row.

A growth stock investor does indeed have the soul of a gambler.

The value investor's soul looks more like that of an accountant. Studies of the two styles show results that are in line with the personalities of their adherents. The growth stock buyer, the gambler, is more likely to strike it rich. The value buyer can get rich, too, but slowly; on average, year by year, he will make a higher return.

Investor, Know Thyself

People do seem to be born with a predilection for one style or the other. It's a matter of personality.

One woman invited to an important party will go to Neiman Marcus and tell the saleslady she wants a knockout outfit, probably by a name designer, something that will make her look marvelous and feel great. Cost is a secondary consideration. The saleslady understands perfectly: "Here's a fantastic dress from Escada. Everybody will recognize it as an Escada, as a beautiful, quality—and expensive—dress. You'll be a great hit." And the woman will pay $1,200 for the dress, go to the party, and indeed feel on top of the world.

Another woman has a totally different response to her invitation. She immediately heads for Loehmann's or Filene's Basement or some other discount-and-remainder emporium, and shops assiduously until she settles on a decent dress for $150. She goes to the party with just as much inner satisfaction as the lady in the couturier outfit. If the first woman can imply, "My marvelous dress shows how much style and money I have, and that makes me feel wonderful," the other woman can respond, "I have a dress that I'll bet cost only a tenth of what's on your back, and mine looks almost as good. I feel great because I'm proud of being imaginative and creative and thrifty."

Two approaches, wholly different, and you can't say one is more valid than the other. Both women are doing what is right for them, and both of the stores they've patronized are commendable in terms of the kind of goods they specialize in.

If you're a Neiman Marcus shopper, you're going to buy Microsoft stock. It may be the greatest company around at the moment, and you will be willing to pay up for that fact. And if you're a Filene's Basement person, you are going to take your time and use your judgment to find a decent-quality stock you believe is a bargain. If you are pursuing a style that doesn't fit your temperament, you won't be happy. Show me an unhappy investor and I'll show you an unsuccessful investor.

Not that the demarcation between growth and value is always crystal clear. A P/E of 15 for any stock might seem high in a bear market and low in a bull market. Sometimes P/Es are no help in fixing value. A cable TV company may have no earnings at all, but if all the other CATV companies are selling at ten times cash flow, that's the way you have to measure its value.

Nor do investors define value in the same way. The value investor says he buys only "undervalued" stocks. That hardly means the growth investor boasts, "And I buy only overvalued stocks." He argues that his stocks, too, are undervalued—that other investors haven't fully factored in the company's glorious growth prospects. He pulls out his stock valuation model to show you that, given future earnings streams, the stock is currently selling for less than its real worth.

Show me an unhappy investor and I'll show you an unsuccessful investor.

After all, growth itself is one component of value. A growing stream of earnings is certainly worth more than a static stream of earnings. You could even say that growth generates value. It can disappear as growth slows, but so can any other part of a value equation. A low P/E, too, can disappear, if earnings shrink. So can a low price-to-book ratio. When I first started in this business, I took a look at steel companies. A large part of their book value was in their open-hearth furnaces, which now, of course, have an economic value of zero. There arc no guarantees for investors, whatever their orientation.

When you come down to it, buying stocks is no different from buying anything else. Price is always a vital determinant in your decision. You can go to the supermarket ready to buy either lobster or chicken. Which shall it be for tonight? A free market will price both so that the market is cleared—sold out—of each at the end of the day. Say the lobster costs $10 a pound and chicken $1 a pound. The store will sell, to pick arbitrary numbers, a dozen lobsters and six hundred chickens. But if lobster suddenly goes from $10 a pound to $30 a pound, the next day you may sell zero lobsters and 615 chickens. If lobster drops to $3 a pound, you'd sell every lobster in sight. People are very conscious of prices and of the relationship between prices and value, and they're quick to shift behavior.

Momentum players buy more lobsters as the price goes up.

It's true in the stock market, too, but the adjustment can take longer, simply because investor behavior can be perverse. So-called momentum players will keep going for the lobster. If the lobster shoots up from $10 a pound to $18 a pound, they'll buy it on the theory that it's going to be $23 a pound in a week. And maybe it will. When people expect inflation and rising costs, they can indeed force prices up, but these are temporary aberrations. In 1980, silver spiked to $40 an ounce. Today it is back to $5. Price bubbles soon burst.

Gender Bender

Investment ideas often come from general reading, and I was struck in 1991 by how much I was reading, in my family newspaper, about sex. It was at that time that the media were busy providing us with lurid anecdotes about Mike Tyson and Desiree Washington, Bill Clinton and Gennifer Flowers, and Clarence Thomas and Anita Hill, as well as clinical details about William Kennedy Smith and Patricia Bowman, a sad story about Magic Johnson and a whole flock of chicks, and a pathetic story about Pee-Wee Herman all by himself.

In all the titillating discussion of sexual harassment in work situations, date rape, condom distribution in schools, abortion, and sexually transmitted diseases, I noted that one important sexual issue had been lost sight of: What does sex do for investors? Does gender matter in the stock market? Might there be a pattern here whose recognition would lead to an investment opportunity?

Our Quantitative Analysis Department went to work and came up with thirteen boy-name stocks and thirteen girl-name stocks.

BOY STOCKS	GIRL STOCKS
Clinton Gas System	Flowers Industries
Thomas Industries	Santa Anita Realty
Smith International	Hills Department Stores
Harman International[1]	Bowmar Instrument[2]
Magic Circle	NUI Corp.[3]
Johnson Products	Claire's Stores
Tyson Foods	Juno Lighting

Mr. Max	Beverly Enterprises
Fred Meyer	Telebras
Edison Brothers	Lindsay Mfg.
He-Ro Group	Ann Taylor
Manpower	Rubbermaid
Thor Industries	Dana Corp.

Some shareholders, by the way, impervious to or unfamiliar with my brand of humor, wrongly took offense at this breakthrough study. We received letters from feminists who thought it demeaning to women. I wasn't picking on women. I was trying to insult everyone equally.

Actually, I was spoofing the foolish studies of quantitative analysts who try to wrap stocks in tidy little packages they declare will react similarly. We at Acorn are never—well, hardly ever—that simplistic.

In any case, three months later, in the first quarter of 1992, we duly reported the results of our sex contest. The girls won. From January 30 through April 30, with dividends included, they had returned 4.5 percent, the boys a mere 0.2 percent (the S&P 500 was up 0.8 percent). This scientific study, we presume, provided proof that will be accepted by all right-thinking people that females are superior in the field of economics.

Having settled that question, Acorn could move on to other, less serious matters.

[1] No stocks named Herman, let alone Pee-Wee.
[2] As close as we could get, or want to get, to Patricia Bowman.
[3] Nui Onoue, a restaurant owner in Osaka, was in the headlines at the time, thanks to her using forged deposit certificates to defraud some major Japanese banks.

Some of Each, Please

I've been called both a value investor and a growth investor. Which I take as a compliment.

There really is no reason to be a pure this or a pure that. I look for what at Acorn we call GARP—growth at a reasonable price. I try to be a sensible shopper. I want good, growing companies, but I don't want to overpay, and I would argue, as I already have, that you have a better chance of finding them among small companies. I seldom buy "supergrowth" stocks, those with 25 or 30 percent growth-in-earnings estimates, because such estimates rarely come true. I also avoid value stocks that have a high stated book value but are in fact very sick companies.

There is a great difference, you know, between the best company and the best stock.

So call me eclectic. I do a little of each. I'm greedy. I want growth at a value price. Just because you like lobster doesn't mean you won't eat chicken. I stick with small-cap stocks, but I don't care if it's a growth idea or a value idea. Or what country it's from. If it looks profitable, I'll do it.

There is a great difference between the best company and the best stock.

The Odds Favor Value

If you put me on the rack, though, and force me to choose one school or the other, I confess to a bias, and it stems from the second law of thermodynamics. Some processes are reversible: you can turn water into steam, which drives an engine, and then turn the steam back into water again. But other processes, says the second law, go in one direction only. After you've mixed a jigger of gin into a glass of tonic water, there is no way you can separate the gin out again. All irreversible processes have one thing in common: the system moves toward a less ordered state. Entropy is the measure of the degree of disorder created.

Let's say you have a stack of pennies, all facing heads up, nice and orderly. Knock over the stack and some of the pennies will fall heads up and some tails up.

Now convert the pennies into stocks. If you sort through a thousand companies and stack, or rank, them according to their growth-in-earnings attractiveness, you'll have a Microsoft or its equivalent at the top and some low-growth dog at the bottom.

Suppose you bought them all and went to the South Seas for a year. Or five years. When you looked at your portfolio again, as with the pennies, you would see randomness, which would be more marked the longer you've been away. Entropy would be evident. Things just don't stay the same.

As time goes on, the top of the list will tend to drift down toward the middle. Growth stocks stumble. (It's a great temptation to buy a venerated name that's 15 percent cheaper than it was last week, but beware. It fell for a reason, probably an earnings disappointment, and one quarter's shortfall is usually followed by more. The Cockroach Theorem applies: "The chance of a company's having one and only one bad quarter is equivalent to the chance of your kitchen's having one and only one cockroach.") When I wrote my undergraduate thesis back in 1955, I chose two companies that were considered among the best in the world: Sears, Roebuck and Inland Steel. The steel industry was thought a high-growth business back then. And Sears dominated retail so completely that nobody could figure out how it could be stopped from taking over the country. Today Inland Steel and Sears, Roebuck may still be profitable, good companies, but if you were making a list of the twenty greatest companies today, I doubt that you'd put either one of them on it.

I can remember when the best stock was Control Data and when the best stock was Burroughs. In the 1950s utilities were considered growth stocks. A hundred years ago, as noted earlier, the best stock, hands down, was the Pennsylvania Railroad. Growth doesn't continue forever.

Or, as I seem to have heard somewhere, trees don't grow to the sky.

A hundred years ago, the best stock was the Pennsylvania Railroad.

Why Don't Trees Grow to the Sky?

That is the sort of nasty question a four-year-old might ask, for it is simple in form but takes some knowledge of science to answer. Luckily, there is a fine resource to consult on the question of why animals and plants have the size and shape that they do. The science classic *On Growth and Form*, by D'Arcy Thompson, is still in print despite its original publication date of nearly eighty years ago. And because it was written in England in 1917, it offers clear English prose instead of matrix algebra.

So, how high can a tree grow? The limit to the height of a tree is governed by its collapse under the force of gravity in a "column failure." The great mathematicians

Euler and Lagrange showed that a column of a certain height would merely be compressed, but one of a greater height would bend under its own weight in any wind load, and then inescapably fall over rather than recover. In 1881, a scientist named Greenhill calculated how a tree-shaped column over a critical height relative to its width would be bent by its own weight. For a typical tree, this would impose a height limit of about three hundred feet. Rand McNally recently stated that the tallest tree ever found was a California redwood measuring 364 feet, quite satisfactorily close to Greenhill's calculation.

I find the fact that trees cannot grow to the sky, because of the effects of gravity on tall slender structures, a useful metaphor, suggesting a limit to the growth of most things, including corporations (also, investment funds, though I am afraid we fund managers cannot blame the force of gravity when our net asset values fall).

In 1990, when the absolute favorite of almost all growth stock investors was Wal-Mart, I took a good look at the stock—though not as a possible investment; it was far too expensive at that point for me. My chance had come earlier, when Wal-Mart was just starting up in Arkansas. A Chicago bank loan officer who specialized in the retail industry suggested I take a look at three discounters, two of them in Arkansas. And I did. Trouble is, neither of the two recommended Arkansas companies was Wal-Mart. They were Sterling Stores and United Dollar, both long bankrupt now. (The loan officer came to a bad end, too, but that's another story.)

By 1990 Wal-Mart had been growing at a 25-percent-per-year clip for a long time. If the chain's expansion rate were to continue, Wal-Mart would be the only retailer left in the country after only twenty-five years. For about five more years Wal-Mart did continue to manage 25 percent a year or better growth. But finally the tree got too high. In fiscal 1996 sales were up only 13.5 percent, and the company that had reported ninety-nine consecutive quarters of earnings growth announced that profits for the fourth quarter of 1995 were down about 10 percent from profits of the year before.

Just as some of the companies on the top of the list will drift downward, some on the bottom will percolate up toward the middle. In statistics this is known as "reversion to the mean."

The high prices investors have paid for the companies originally at the top of the list will prove disastrous if those companies' earnings prove below analysts' forecasts, and since analysts consistently overestimate growth rates, disasters happen all the time. A 20 percent growth rate is a nice round number, easy for an analyst to pencil in, and that gets people excited. It should, because 20 percent growth over time would be spectacular. And at some point, impossible to sustain.

Earnings disappointments aren't as rough on value stocks, because they're already in the basement. More important, some of them come through with surprises on the upside, which propels them smartly up the list.

The skilled growth stock manager will continually restore the integrity of his list. But the probabilities, the odds, the very laws of nature are tilted in favor of the value school. Some three dozen published academic studies have shown that, indeed, over long periods, value investors, culling from the bottom of the list, have tended to outperform growth investors. As one example, Professors Richard Thaler of Cornell and Werner De Bondt of the University of Wisconsin constructed sets of portfolios of the fifty best- and worst-performing stocks on the New York Stock Exchange over five-year periods. In each following five-year period the losers outpaced the winners by about 40 percent.

Some three dozen academic studies show that over long periods value investors earn better returns than growth investors.

The further once-venerated growth stocks fall down the ranking, the more interesting they become to value investors. "Fallen angels," they're called in the business. IBM was the growth stock of growth stocks until the future of its mainframe business came into question. Before long the growth boys were throwing out the stock and the value crew was catching it, in part because by then it was paying a 5 percent dividend. The drug stocks were the darlings of the growth camp until the Clintons decided to reinvent our health care system and Merck, Pfizer, Eli Lilly, and the rest got cheap enough for the value investors to begin feasting on them.

But just as growth stocks don't grow forever, value stocks, too, have their flaws. For very often the thing valued turns out to be ephemeral. You bought a stock that was trading at half book value and it turns out the book value evaporates, as was true of the open-hearth furnaces on the balance sheets of the steel companies. Or inventory turns out to be worth less than projected. Or, more fundamentally, the stock is cheap because the company is sick, and instead of recovering, as the value buyer expected, the patient dies.

Still, Valueland is probably a better place to live in over the long term. And just as some growth stocks stumble and turn into fallen-angel value stocks, some value stocks blossom into growth stocks. The greatest investment satisfaction of all is to see an ugly duckling recognized as a swan.

My favorite ugly duckling stock is Newell Industries. It's in the most mundane businesses you could imagine. It makes frying pans, knitting needles, curtain rods and drapery hooks, paint rollers, a whole catalog of routine hardware and home decorating items. We're not dealing with integrated circuits here. I've owned Newell since 1984, paying as little as $1.68 (adjusted for splits) a share for it. Since nobody could get excited by paint rollers and drapery hooks, the stock was cheap, a value bet for sure.

The greatest investment profit comes when an ugly duckling becomes a swan.

But Newell is a superbly run company, tremendously cost conscious and an aggressive marketer. It delivers low-cost, quality goods on time. The Taiwanese can't beat it on price or delivery. What's more, it has shown an uncanny ability to buy other companies, apply its magic, and make them equally profitable. When Wall Street finally realized that Newell was literally wired (through computer network linkage) into Wal-Mart and Home Depot, the transformation to swan was certified and the stock took off. The stock's been as high as $32. Ideally one should buy the stock of a small company below its economic value and sell it at its full economic value when it has grown into a proven success, but Newell still has some great years ahead.

Grand Slams

Finding ugly ducklings that turn into swans, like Newell, and that bring you five or ten or more times your money is a very good idea indeed. When people ask me how we've managed to get our results, I tell them that it's not by avoiding disasters, because I have had my share of them. That's understood with small-cap investing. But if you manage to own some stocks that go up ten times, that pays for a lot of the disasters, with profits left over.

Newell hasn't been Acorn's only big winner. Harley-Davidson, Hillenbrand, IMS International, and a few others have turned into ten-baggers. But three blockbusters did even better. They superbly illustrate that someone who is careful about price can still win the biggest trophies.

HOUSTON OIL & MINERALS

The first one, which kept the fund alive at a critical juncture, came into the fund in 1973. A friend in New York, Perry Swenson, who worked at a small brokerage firm named Wood Walker (now Legg Mason Wood Walker Inc.), told me to go to the Union League Club and listen to a talk by the president of Houston Oil & Minerals, a tiny gas exploration company in Texas. The market was dreary at the time, the meeting was in the afternoon, and most people, after two scotches, fell asleep. But I listened and liked what I heard: Houston Oil had just found a very large gas field in Galveston Bay that could transform the company.

I took a large position in the stock, starting in the second quarter of 1973, and in the third quarter it moved from $28 to $67, then split two for one. Wall Street finally caught on that the Galveston Bay discovery would soon result in an enormous increase in earnings. I held on to Houston for years. By the middle of 1977, a stock that cost $220,000 was worth, after numerous splits, $5.3 million.

It had risen by a factor of twenty-four. The whole fund had only $43 million at the time, so a profit of that size was very meaningful. I think that without Houston Oil we would have been blown out like a candle in the 1973–74 bear market. Many funds were.

CRAY RESEARCH

Twenty years ago the late Seymour Cray was the most famous computer designer in the country. When his company, Cray Research, went public in 1978, I wondered whether we ought to invest in it, because it was quite speculative. But then I told myself, "This is like being asked to invest with Thomas Edison or Henry Ford. Cray is one of the great minds of the century, and if you invest with him and you lose money, it's just one more loss; you'll get over it. But if you don't invest with him and the company proves successful, you'll never forgive yourself."

On that basis, I bought a considerable amount of stock. Seven years later, after three splits, we had fifteen times as many shares as we started with, and our $1.5 million investment had a market value of $20 million.

> The fact that a stock has already moved up sharply doesn't mean that it can't still have plenty of room left to climb.

Interestingly, we had an offer to get into Cray on a venture capital basis a year before it went public, but we turned it down. As I explained in the last chapter, venture capital involves more risk than I want to take, and Cray hadn't actually built his first machine yet. The stock tripled between the time of the venture capital financing and the original public offering. But that shows that if a business is good enough, the fact that its stock has already moved up doesn't mean that there can't still be plenty of room left to climb.

INTERNATIONAL GAME TECHNOLOGY

International Game Technology is now the world's leading maker of slot machines, but back in 1988, when I first bought it, it was, on the whole, a broken-down company. No Wall Street analyst had anything good to say about it. It was considered a low-growth capital goods supplier to a cyclical industry. The stock was cheap, a value play for sure.

But a bit of homework convinced me that gambling was going to be a very good business around the world. Beyond that, new owners had just taken over International Game, and they were transforming the company. From a maker of routine mechanical slot machines, IGT was turning into the creator of high-tech electronic slots that require almost no maintenance and allow casinos to hook up machines (so they can offer "Megabucks" jackpots), add lottery components, and introduce other novel games. The company hadn't just improved on its old machines; it had introduced something excitingly new.

I paid roughly the current equivalent of $1 a share, which was about ten times International Game's trailing twelve months' earnings. Then the earnings went up ten times and the P/E went up four times, and I ended up with forty times my original money. By the time the stock reached its high of $40 in 1993, it had most definitely turned into a growth stock. Eventually, gambling issues went from craze-of-the-day to so-what-else-is-new stocks, and the P/E dropped in half.

Making forty times your money is a very pleasant experience. I highly recommend it.

Investing in small companies is a little like baseball. Whenever you come up to bat, you always hope for a grand slam. Babe Ruth struck out often, but his home run record is legendary. If you take enough swings, you, too, will watch a few go over the wall.

You never know which stocks will clear the fence. Every stock we've bought came with a great story. More often than not we're surprised by events, and the surprises happen in both directions. "Sure winners" often disappoint, and some of the companies with seemingly more modest futures turn into powerhouses.

But one fact is undeniable: you can't make five or ten or twenty times your money if you don't hold on to stocks. Most people are delighted when a stock doubles, and quickly sell to lock in their gain. If a company is still performing, let its stock, too, continue to perform.

4

▰▰▰▰▰▰▰▰▰▰▰▰▰▰▰▰▰▰▰▰

BAD NEWS BULLS

Value stocks have another attraction: they are constantly in fresh production. A new batch often appears when the troubles of a few leaders taint a whole industry.

Bad news usually gets exaggerated, and not just in the investment world, of course. What happened in the late 1970s, after the United States launched its first manned space station, called Skylab, seemed to me at the time a perfect metaphor for the way investors overreact to bad news, thus creating opportunities for the few who stay levelheaded. I still know no better example.

After a few years in orbit Skylab began to decay, and it was clear that it was going to fall back into the atmosphere. Hysteria erupted: the press reveled in stories intimating that all our lives were threatened by debris. *Time* devoted a cover story to the impending disaster. I'm sure thousands of little children hid under their beds.

"Wait a minute," I said to myself; "journalists don't know anything about probabilities. They are opposed to numbers." And the average person, no better acquainted with statistics,* thoroughly

---

*One study found the public believes accidents cause as many deaths as diseases. The truth is, diseases take about fifteen times as many lives.

exaggerates the probability of long-shot events, treating chances that may be one in a thousand as though they were one in twenty. So I started to calculate the odds of harm emanating from five hundred lethal pieces, about the size of .50-caliber bullets, falling on 5 billion people over 510 million square kilometers of inhabited earth.

By my calculation, the odds of your staying alive during Skylab's fall were actually not too bad. If five hundred lumps should fall out of the sky at random, the odds of any piece hitting anyone in the world would be about one in two hundred, and of hitting any American, one in three thousand. In fact, NASA had some ability to control Skylab's landing area, so that the odds against an American fatality must have been about twenty thousand to one. Since about 130 Americans were killed in motor vehicle accidents every day that year, the chance of an American's being killed in a car on July 11, 1979, was four hundred thousand times greater than the chance of being killed by Skylab.

Skylab did break up in the atmosphere, but the pieces landed, as NASA had planned, in the Indian Ocean, which is about the least populated part of the world. Few of the pieces even fell on land. Maybe a few Australian sheep were mildly disturbed, but there were certainly no human casualties. The whole thing was a joke.

Three Mile Island, which blew up about the same time that Skylab fell down, was another example of absurd overreaction. The reactor was trashed, but the containment vessel stayed intact and kept the radioactive debris sealed up. The International Atomic Energy Agency report found that no radiation was released outside the plant (unlike at Chernobyl, which had no containment vessel). The press so exaggerated the scope of the damage that millions of Americans are convinced that a major public health disaster occurred.

The truth was quite different. Suppose you had twins, both living on a farm on the edge of Three Mile Island. One fellow was worried sick, so he got in his car and drove off toward Harrisburg in a panic. But the other twin said, "Bosh, I've had enough of this stuff," and took off all his clothes and stood right next to Three Mile Island for a day. Who took the greater risk? You could easily show that it was the twin who drove off, because the chance of being killed in a car accident was much higher than it was for the fellow standing there naked.

But the combined hysterics of the media and the politicians had their effect: the U.S. nuclear power industry ended at Three Mile Island. No matter that other energy sources, including coal, synthetic fuels, and even solar power, are each damaging to the environment in their own way and carry a much higher risk of human deaths.

The Mental Factor

Popular reactions to real or imagined disasters have been studied thoroughly. Books have been written, for example, about the panic that followed Orson Welles's radio drama *The War of the Worlds*, which convinced a good part of the population that Martians had invaded New Jersey. But it wasn't until the early 1980s that psychologists began to take a look at how people respond to *financial* anxieties. When they finally did, they found that the same kind of irrationality prevails.

> There is a steady flow of wealth from hopeful gamblers to the men who know what the odds really are.

Much of the pioneering work was done by the late Amos Tversky, a professor at Stanford, and Daniel Kahneman, now at Princeton. Their studies confirmed that in money matters, too, most people exaggerate the likelihood of occurrences. If something can happen, then it must be a concern, whether the probability of the event is one in a thousand or one in a million. This explains the popularity of cancer insurance, flight insurance, and other forms of protection against catastrophes, even though the policies cost far more than an actuarially fair price.

People overestimate the value of a chance on a long-shot win just as much as they blow up the dangers of rare, spectacular events. Gambling casinos, racetracks, and lotteries are always busy. There is a steady flow of wealth from hopeful gamblers to the men who know what the odds really are.

This phenomenon is verifiably true in the case of call options on stocks. Very-low-priced options sell for higher prices than their valuations based on probability theory would suggest, because they are like lottery tickets. Sensible investors should avoid, too, very-low-priced, very risky stocks. Two-dollar "bargain" stocks are probably overpriced, despite—or because of—their very low price. W. C. Fields, in *The Bank Dick*, hit it rich in Beefsteak Mines stock, but long-shot investments are poor bets in real life.

One of Tversky and Kahneman's major discoveries was that a dollar of gain is not equal to a dollar lost in most people's minds, certainly not when the dollar stake is high. Who would bet his car against a neighbor's similar car at even odds? Very few, because having no car is more of a bad than having two cars is a good. Formally, the value function is nonlinear, so that individuals have more displeasure in losing a sum than the pleasure associated with winning the same amount. Most people want a two-thirds chance of winning to venture a big bet.

If most investors act in this risk-averse way, we can understand why they will accept a lower return from bonds and other fixed-income investments rather than hold stocks, and why they will stick with the blue chips instead of taking a chance on capturing the higher returns of small-company stocks. I know that when I find a situation where it seems to me probabilities favor the rewards over the risks, I will have no trouble finding the other side of the trade, because most people ignore probabilities, exaggerate the risks, and are prone to sacrifice returns in favor of perceived safety.

Most people ignore probabilities and exaggerate risks.

One of the more interesting aspects of the Kahneman and Tversky studies deals with the role of context in the decision-making process. People make up their minds differently according to how a problem is presented to them. Perversely, when the potential gain in a transaction is stressed, people get nervous and wary; and when potential losses are played up, they are so spooked they are willing to assume what are in reality greater risks in order to avoid the losses.

For example, suppose a person has spent an afternoon at the racetrack, has lost $140, and is considering a $10 bet on a fifteen-to-one long shot in the last race. This decision can be framed in two ways, which correspond to two natural reference points. If the reference point is restricted to the bettor's current cash on hand, the outcomes of the bet are framed as a gain of $140 *or* a loss of $10. On the other hand, it may be more natural to view the present state as a loss of $140 for the betting day, and accordingly frame the last bet as a chance to get back to even *or* to increase the loss a mere $10. Prospect theory implies that the latter frame of reference will produce more risk seeking than the former. Hence, people who do not adjust their reference point as they lose can be expected to make bets they would normally find outrageous, even on a dubious nag at fifteen to one. This analysis is confirmed by the observation that bets on long shots are most popular on the last race of the day.

The same thing happens to stock investors who have a loss on a stock. Unable to face the reality of what the stock is now actually worth, the unlucky owner is willing to take a sucker bet by holding on to the stock, even when he knows the company's in trouble, in the wild hope of a comeback that will erase his loss. The stock market is not a racetrack, but we do know that investors behave differently in bull and bear markets, and framing theory helps explain part of the difference.

In recent years academic studies of financial behavior—and, more specifically, investor behavior—have proliferated. In April 1995, for example, the financial analysts' professional organization, the Association of Investment Management and Research (AIMR), sponsored a conference titled "Behavioral Finance and Decision Theory in Investment Management." Half a dozen researchers (Tversky, who died about a year later, among them) presented papers. In May 1996, at Harvard, money managers mixed with academics for a two-day seminar on "behavioral economics." One message of this latter meeting was that people get carried away by, and pay too much for, glamorous growth stocks; this led to several endorsements of value investing as a superior strategy.

The more recent studies only confirm the original conclusion, that investors—like all humans—react to situations in ways that are not totally rational or even necessarily in their own best interest, contrary to what classical economics had assumed. Investors must consider economic and corporate events, of course, but much that moves markets and individual stocks extends beyond interest rates and earnings per share. The efficient-market hypothesis largely depends on the thesis that investors react to new information in a rational way. The psychologists' challenge of that assumption has bolstered the claim investment professionals have made for years: investors assess information emotionally, creating price distortions that the astute and nimble can exploit.

Overdiscounting

Skylab, Three Mile Island, and studies of investor psychology all dramatize an important moneymaking message: there are sound companies with a small probability of trouble that become good buys when the market is too fearful of improbable disasters. When something negative happens, a stock may go down much more than the news warrants. This happens so often that it has its own name: "overdiscounting bad news."

Investors assess information emotionally, creating price distortions that the astute and nimble can exploit.

Opportunities among individual stocks can pop up at any time after such overreactions. Just about the time of Skylab and Three Mile Island, as a matter of fact, a terrible DC-10 crash at Chicago's O'Hare Airport sent McDonnell Douglas stock from 28 to 20. After the shock wore off a little, the stock recovered to 26. That kind of sell-off and bounce back is particularly common today, because of the increasing popularity of so-called momentum investing. Momentum managers buy stocks almost solely on the basis of their recent market rise—they show "relative strength," is the way the managers prefer to describe it—and then sell them if the price drops by some predetermined amount, like 15 percent from a high. (One could say that's not a bad description of someone who buys high and sells low.) Because the system works relatively well in the latter stages of a bull market, it has attracted ever more adherents and assets in the 1990s, and since momentum practitioners all buy the same hot stocks and dump them at the same time when any bit of bad news triggers their sell disciplines, these stocks can be sent plunging well below realistic values.

What also happens with regularity is that a whole industry or sector is knocked down to bargain levels by exaggerated apprehensions. Whenever investors fear disaster for an industry, you can find sound companies, with little risk, at knocked-down prices.

There's no better example than the banking industry over the last dozen years or so. The big money center banks have been in continual trouble because of their willingness—nay, eagerness—to lend money to dubious credits. (In my opinion, "aggressive banker" should be an oxymoron, like "aggressive mistress.") Back in 1982–83 the so-called sovereign loans were in the headlines. The banks kept rolling over the debts owed by tardy government borrowers like Argentina, Brazil, Poland, Zaire, and Mexico. (We were worried about a Mexican default in the first quarter of 1983 and we were worried about a Mexican default in the first quarter of 1995; the same old problems often return again and again.) Government defaults and refinancings were then compounded by shaky loans to shaky real estate developers and, to a lesser degree, leveraged buyout firms.

The big-city banks had brought real problems on themselves, no doubt of that. But the little bank in Wilmington, Delaware, or Honolulu that had no sovereign loans on its books and had been very careful in its real estate lending got tarred with the same brush of imprudence as the big international players. Its stock became markedly undervalued. We bought quite a few of those banks

The Credulous Tailor

While pondering the bad-loan headaches of the banking industry a few years back, I was able to locate a world-class loan rollover artist in the person of the Professor in *Sylvie and Bruno*, a book by Lewis Carroll, of *Alice* fame.

The Professor's twisted logic fits modern banking theory nicely. There is a knock on the door, and the Professor shouts, "Come in!"

"Only the tailor, Sir, with your little bill," said a meek voice outside the door.

"Ah, well, I can soon settle *his* business," the Professor said to the children, "if you'll just wait a minute. How much is it, this year, my man?" The tailor had come in while he was speaking.

"Well, it's been doubling so many years, you see," the tailor replied, a little gruffly, "and I think I'd like to see the money now. It's two thousand pounds, it is!"

"Oh, that's nothing!" the Professor carelessly remarked, feeling in his pocket, as if he always carried at least that amount about with him. "But wouldn't you like to wait just another year, and make it *four* thousand? Just think how rich you'd be! Why, you might be a *King*, if you liked!"

"I don't know as I'd care about being a *King*," the man said thoughtfully, "but it *dew* sound a powerful sight o' money! Well, I think I'll wait—"

"Of course you will!" said the Professor. "There's good sense in you, I see. Good-day to you, my man!"

"Will you ever have to pay him that four thousand pounds?" Sylvie asked as the door closed on the departing creditor.

"*Never*, my child!" the Professor replied emphatically. "He'll go on doubling it, til he dies. You see, it's always worth while waiting another year, to get twice as much money!"

Carroll's book was published in 1889, and since death does not occur in this fantasy world, I assume that the Professor and the tailor kept up their annual rollover exercise, which means that the tailor's "little bill" is now valued in uncountable trillions of dollars. And it continues to double every year, which means that this little unknown tailor is surely the largest creditor in all fiction and is, if the accountant will certify his receivables as collectable, the wealthiest character ever invented.

One wonders if the tailor's real problem was that he was in the wrong line of work. He should have resigned from the book and obtained a job in the loan department of a big bank, where he could soon have made a name for himself (which he badly needs, for Carroll leaves him nameless). He has already mastered the art of rollover and understands about penalty interest rates; his rate is 100 percent per year, which he has learned to take into his income statement, at least as psychic income. His loan is perfectly sound, for there is no risk of default by the Professor—unless, of course, the tailor were unwise enough to finally write off his folly.

(making sure they were the ones run by bankers, not tailors—see accompanying box). Sooner or later, we figured—and we proved right—investors would pay more for these low-P/E bank stocks, for, as I asked Acorn's shareholders, "How ya gonna keep 'em down on these firms after they've seen P/Es?"

The same thing happened when the savings and loan scandal erupted. Everyone was mourning the death of the industry, but we concluded that at least a few S&Ls had to survive, like buffalo herds in Yellowstone National Park. We bought the stocks of several perfectly sound savings banks on the cheap and made out very well.

We had another chance at the bargain table in July 1996, when a couple of technology companies announced that earnings would be lower than consensus estimates and, in the ensuing panic, high-tech stocks were thrown out the window en masse. Many of the stocks had been hoisted to ridiculous levels by the momentum players and were probably still expensive even at 50 percent markdowns. But some good, reasonably priced companies quickly became unreasonably cheap companies. When the hysteria subsided, their stocks climbed back up.

Note that we want the *sound* banks and *good* companies. When an industry gets bombed, you can't pick indiscriminately from the rubble. But research will usually turn up some legitimate bargains. Then all it takes is patience.

5

████████████████████████████████

ON YOUR OWN, OR CALL IN THE EXPERTS?

My Uncle David made out very well in the stock market.

He had nothing to do with the securities industry. He was in retailing (small-town women's clothing stores), and the only stocks he bought were those of companies in the businesses he knew—other retailers, apparel manufacturers, and suppliers to the industry. He could judge these companies' products, pricing, and distribution muscle, and he knew what was key to look for in their financial statements, particularly any changes in inventories, cash flows, and bank debt. Sometimes he knew managements personally and had strong opinions about their ability and honesty.

But his main edge was that he knew store buyers. Goods ordered aren't manufactured and shipped until months later, so by chatting with buyers, he had a fairly good idea in March what kind of earnings the clothing makers would be reporting in September and December. Buying into businesses he understood, he made a good deal of money over more than a half century in the market.

Whether you are attracted to the growth or the value school of investing—Uncle David probably never even thought about such labels—you first have to make the big decision: are you, like my uncle, going to build a portfolio yourself, or are you going to turn the job over to a professional? That professional could be an investment counselor, or in a bank trust department, or a broker entrusted with discretionary power. But for most people, hiring a professional means buying the shares of a mutual fund.

Investing is like a lot of other skills. You can fix your own sink, you can write your own will, and you can buy your own stocks. You may do fine, as my uncle did. And, like him, you may get pleasure out of it.

I know people who are marvelous carpenters or gardeners or amateur electricians. They enjoy puttering and repairing; it's their hobby. Well, investing is a lovely hobby. It can be pursued in any weather. It has no health or age restrictions. There is no end to the hours you can spend on it. You read interesting publications and hear the opinions of exceedingly bright and persuasive people. And it's one leisure-time activity you don't have to conceal from your spouse.

There's no magic in security analysis. Its practitioners aren't members of some mystery cult. It's just a question of trying to understand what's going to happen to a company in the next few years. If you know an industry, as Uncle David did, you have an advantage, and that's where you should look. If you know the insurance business and think that you therefore know enough about business in general to also buy computer stocks, you'll probably find out that you've lost your edge.

The further you stray from stocks you really understand, the more likely you are gambling rather than investing.

Which leads me to a basic rule for stock investors: find out what you know and what you don't know. The further you stray from stocks you really understand, the more likely it is that you are gambling rather than investing.

Mutual funds can't give you the same sense of participation as on-your-own investing. Or of excitement, for direct investing is a bit of a game—a search for clues that can reveal where the treasure's hidden. It can be a very expensive hobby if you're not careful. But if you're good at it, you can enjoy yourself and make money at the same time.

Get Yourself a Style

If you do decide to invest on your own—with a broker as your Virgilian guide through our underworld—the most important advice I can give you is that you need to have a strategy, a way of looking at the world of stocks. That might seem like an unnecessary truism, but if you examine the portfolios of most do-it-themselfers, you find a hodgepodge—a stock a friend said he heard is going to be involved in a takeover, a company that *Forbes* reported has a fabulous new widget, a stock that's dropped so far in price that your broker's told you it's a steal, the stock of a restaurant chain where you had a surprisingly good and cheap steak last week. In other words, a haphazard collection of *stories.*

Successful investors don't operate that way. They have a philosophy that dictates what kind of stocks they want to own, and they stick to their catechism. When you think of the best-known names in the business—John Templeton, Warren Buffett, Peter Lynch, and John Neff as examples—you can immediately attach an investment style to each. I know the main reason that Acorn's done well is that we've had a philosophy, a strategy, a set of values, a discipline—call it what you will—that has kept us on a constant path over the years.

I have always sought smaller companies that are understandable, with a dominant market position in whatever they make or do, which means they are usually in only one or two lines of business. We like entrepreneurial management, which is common among small companies, and financial strength, which is not, but I don't want to be involved with risky start-ups or turnaround situations. And the stocks still have to be on the cheap side, usually because they aren't as yet very well known.

I haven't strayed from that investment philosophy since I first articulated it to shareholders over a quarter century ago. I like to think I've learned a thing or two over the decades, but I haven't changed my basic approach. I still want to load the shopping cart with cheap stocks of small, sound companies with products or services in demand—increasingly, in worldwide demand. An investor's view of markets can be valid for a very long time. I like to believe, too, that I've practiced what I've preached. When you deviate from what you know and do best, you usually get into trouble. Good investors are those who have a vision and stick to it.

A mutual fund, particularly a small-company fund, can have one problem the individual isn't going to face. If it does well and money floods in, it becomes harder to adhere to its original declarations. But it can be done. Some of our companies are larger than those we bought at the beginning, and we own more positions, but the selection criteria haven't changed. But I know a small-cap fund can get too large. Wanger Asset Management's logo is the squirrel, and you don't see many three-hundred-pound squirrels in the park.

When you invest through mutual funds, you can own a value fund and a growth fund, a big-company and a small-company fund. But when you're investing on your own, you can't spread yourself into all corners. Aside from the size of the portfolio you'd need to achieve such diversity, you'd never develop and hone a style of your own.

Too often people start with a discipline but abandon it. And it's like virginity: if you lose it when you're eighteen, you may never find it again. It's so easy to let yourself be caught up in the market enthusiasms of the day. Every force in the world—the "experts" quoted in the papers and on TV and radio, your broker, newsletters, a golf buddy—is hammering on you to get on this or that bandwagon. It's time to buy high-tech or cyclicals or brand-name growth stocks or utilities or Latin America or China. All too often you end up buying the hot sector at the peak of its cycle.

Too often people start with a discipline but abandon it.

If instead you develop a set of convictions you adhere to, you can turn your back on thousands of stocks and concentrate on a manageable universe. A set of guidelines—and I urge you to put them down on paper—gives you confidence when times are rough. It helps you make the toughest decisions: when to sell. It makes it possible to get better and better through cultivation of a repeated skill. And it keeps you from the folly of the amateur who leaps from fad to fad, usually just about the time the fad is fading.

But it has to be *your* strategy, what's right for you. Every singer must sing her own song.

Risk Is in the Eyes of the Beholder

The truth is, we all have an investment philosophy, even if we don't know it. In general, it was formed by the time we were out of sixth grade. Because the main question an investor has to ask himself or herself is, "What is my attitude toward risk?" And that probably hasn't changed since you were twelve years old.

That attitude is so ingrained and instinctive that if you try to do something contrary to it, you won't be comfortable, and why should you use your money to make yourself uncomfortable? If you are not a risk taker but you chase fast-growing small companies because you've been told that's where the big money is, you'll be dismayed by the stocks' gyrations, hate what you are doing, and probably make a mess of it. The converse is just as true: if you *are* a risk taker and you end up with a plateful of municipal bonds because some financial planner advised it, you'll also be miserable.

The main question an investor has to ask himself is, "What is my attitude toward risk?" And that probably hasn't changed since you were twelve years old.

So the first thing to do is find out who you are. If philosophic wisdom begins with the admonition "Know thyself," then financial wisdom begins with "Know thy risk tolerance." For instance, an equity fund like mine, which concentrates on small-company stocks, is volatile. A risk-averse person will never be wholly comfortable owning it. A very risk-averse person probably shouldn't be in stocks at all, but should stick to fixed-income investments.

There are tests you can take to establish your risk quotient—the kind you find in some investment cookbooks—but if you ponder it and are honest with yourself, you know your tolerance for risk.

Deciding on an investment philosophy is kind of like picking a spouse. Do you want someone who is volatile and romantic and emotional, or do you want someone who is steady and trustworthy and down to earth? We all have friends who have been long and happily hitched to people we can't stand to be in the same room with for fifteen minutes. If you want a successful investment career, you'd better bind yourself to a style you can live with.

Be faithful. So many investors repeatedly switch into the investment strategy that worked last year. Chasing whatever group of stocks has already gone up, they are forever being whipsawed.

I believe, moreover, that investors intuitively understand not only their own tolerance for risk but the innate riskiness of the different investments and approaches available to them. If Bert made 20 percent on his money speculating in soybean futures, while Betty made only a 10 percent return holding government bonds, most people would say that Bert's superior profit required taking much more risk than they'd be comfortable with, and that they'd be happier with Betty's safe return.

Lessons from the Trenches

If you adhere to a philosophy, you'll avoid the trouble that comes from chasing fads. I've watched a slew of them soar and fizzle.

When I was just starting out in this business, in 1961, defense electronics were the rage. There was an initial public offering (IPO) boom that has probably not been equaled since for low quality. A flood of underwritings launched companies whose future growth prospects were ballyhooed as sensational, and the stocks would go to huge premiums above the original issue price. Price risk was ignored.

A hot-deal market can never sustain itself for long, and we had the short but steep bear market of 1962. Whatever number of those companies were still in business—and many were not—their stock prices plummeted. Another new-issue wave swept over investors in 1968, but was broken by the 1970 bear market. Enthusiasm for IPOs always surges in mature bull markets; we saw it again in 1996, when IPO issuance reached record levels.

After the 1968–70 new-issue binge and bust, investors decided that only big growth companies counted, and we soon had the day of the "one-decision" growth stocks selling at seventy-five times earnings that we talked about in the first chapter. The bear market of 1973–74 ended that phase with a bang. Now growth was hated. Low risk and the supposed safety of high-yield dividends were all that mattered.

I had watched investors chase first after the new-issue market, then the Nifty Fifty, and then the high-dividend payers. I just lashed myself to the mast of Growth at a Fair Price and thereby escaped the siren songs of junky new issues and stocks selling at astronomical P/Es, surviving to enjoy the bargains left in the wake of 1973–74. Since 1982 the market has generally swept upward, but not without severe corrections, particularly among sectors that swelled to crazy valuations. Investors constantly rotating their portfolios to catch the dazzling performers of the moment have had disappointing results in an extraordinary bull market. A philosophy is important not in the abstract but because it will keep you on the right track.

It will also empower you to shut your ears to opportunistic brokers enticing you to switch into the hot style of the moment. Brokers earn a living only when you move your money around, and Wall Street knows how to trumpet the latest fad. In 1976 Benjamin Graham, the inventor of security analysis, summed up his observations after sixty years in the market:

> They used to say about the Bourbons that they forgot nothing. I'll say about the Wall Street people, typically, that they learn nothing, and they forget everything. I have no confidence whatever in the future behavior of the Wall Street people.

Hiring a Pro

Considering the time and discipline investing demands, the skills and knowledge and resources it takes, and the kind of personality it requires, I've long been convinced that mutual funds are the sensible course for 95 percent of investors.

Is that because I'm in the mutual fund business? No, I'm not hustling. Running mutual funds may be my line of work, but I am not trying to drum up business. I just think most people will do better in funds than on their own.

Considering the time, discipline, skills, knowledge, resources, and personality that investing demands, mutual funds are the sensible course for 95 percent of the public.

Most fundamentally, mutual funds give you instant diversification, which means they are the *only* way to go if you don't have at least $100,000 to put into the market. Diversification, of course, lowers risk. The more concentrated a portfolio, by sector and stocks, the more you can hit it big if your call is right. If it's wrong, it's you that will get hit. The biggest risk takers usually invest on their own, because then they can put all their chips on just a handful of numbers. Again, know thyself.

Mutual funds, as just noted, also allow you to diversify in many directions—to have your money with growth and value managers, in small and large companies, and in foreign companies. This kind of diversification also lowers risk and smooths out returns year to year, and in the long run provides better returns.

But the main argument for mutual funds, to my mind, is that your money is managed by a full-time professional. Over the years I've been very impressed with the people in the mutual fund industry. It's a classy bunch of intelligent, well-educated, hardworking, and dedicated people. (I'm the only one who doesn't take the job seriously.)

Professionalism means more than a graduate degree in finance. The fund manager has experience: He's lived through good and bad markets and learned from both. He's spent years building contacts in industry and on Wall Street, and so have his colleagues in the firm. Professionals know where to turn for critical information. And they have clout. How-to investment books often advise individual investors to call up a company they're interested in to get information, but even if you overcome shyness and make the call, you talk to an investment relations officer. The fund manager and analyst get the skinny from the top brass.

The main argument for mutual funds is that your money is managed by a full-time professional.

Professionalism means expertise, and I mean beyond the ability to read balance sheets. Uncle David knew apparel manufacturing and retailing, but that sharply limited his investment horizon. To a large degree the key to recognizing exceptional growth opportunities in our day depends on an understanding of technology. It's important in evaluating not just computer, telecommunications, and software companies but almost every kind of manufacturing company, health care company, and other product and service firms. Since my undergraduate degree was in engineering, I am comfortable with technology matters, and I believe that has benefited my shareholders. At other funds the manager may have to rely on someone on the research staff or an outside consultant, but the knowledge is at hand.

Every business has its own jargon, and the ability to command some of that jargon when talking to people is extremely helpful. I remember once visiting a company that made valves for chemical plants, and the chief engineer was largely giving me the brush-off. He was polite but he didn't think that I, a suit from the city, would understand anything about manufacturing processes. Then I asked him, "Do you get much porosity in your castings?" "Porosity," a word I remembered from a metallurgy course, opened the engineer up like magic. He said to himself, "My God, a Wall Street dude who understands something about the foundry business." After that I couldn't stop him from explaining every last detail about his factory.

Every mutual fund company of any size has a team of analysts who are familiar with all sorts of businesses and their jargons, not to mention foreign languages and cultures. No one person can know everything it would be ideal to know as an investor, for there is no field of human knowledge that isn't valuable somewhere in the investment process. Obviously, you have to know finance and economics, but you also have to know technology and marketing and accounting and statistics and psychology and engineering. Even history and political science are valuable. It would be hard to find some field of knowledge you couldn't apply. So a mutual fund company's team of portfolio managers and analysts, each of whom contributes an area of expertise or two, is extremely valuable in putting together a portfolio.

> You can't know everything you would like to know as an investor, for there is no field of human knowledge that isn't valuable somehow.

When you invest on your own, you deal with one broker, maybe a couple. A mutual fund manager can tap dozens. Acorn works with Merrill Lynch and the other majors, of course, but many of our best stock ideas have come from smaller, regional firms that spot interesting companies in their own backyard. You've probably never even heard of most of these firms—names like Hanifen, Imhoff; Volpe, Welty; Johnston-Lemon; the Buckingham Research Group; Principal Financial Securities; Cleary Gull Reiland & McDevitt; and Adams Harkness & Hill. We also work with brokers in London, Frankfurt, Tokyo, Hong Kong, and other foreign centers. And when we're sold on a company, we buy thousands of shares of its stock, which means we get more attention—from brokers, investment bankers, and companies—than you as an individual could possibly command unless your name is Bill Gates.

A Guide Recommended

Investing in foreign stocks is particularly hard to do on your own. You may know a good deal about what's happening around your town that could lead to investment ideas, but you probably aren't up to date about what's going on in Finland, and even if you're fine in Finland, I'd be very surprised if you also know what's transpiring in Thailand. And even if you know a lot about countries, you'll find it tough to find out about companies that you can invest in. You can usually manage to scrape up most of the information you want on U.S. companies, but overseas it can be tough to find out even the basics.

A couple of years ago, to build our files, we wrote to several hundred companies abroad, asking them to send us their annual and interim reports. We got about a 15 percent response rate. Companies over there may not even have someone who's responsible for shareholders and potential shareholders—no one had been designated to open investors' letters. The only way to secure reports in many countries is to write or call the particular broker who handles the company's investor inquiries.

Information is only one of the problems when you look abroad, and all of the problems are exaggerated when you deal in emerging markets. Clearing and settlement can take weeks. Errors in reporting trades are common and difficult to set right. Insider trading, usually allowed abroad, makes you feel you're competing under a handicap. "Financial reports," as *The Wall Street Journal* recently noted, "if they come at all, may not be in English." The currency exposure and deciding whether or not to hedge that exposure and how to carry out the hedging are other important issues. I can assure you that Southeast Asia and Latin America are not places in which the average individual should try to invest by calling up PaineWebber and placing an order. Buying stocks out there is an invitation to a nightmare. There should be a disclaimer, like those you used to see in TV commercials: "This was done by a professional stunt driver. Kids: Don't try this at home!"

Southeast Asia and Latin America are not good places for the average individual to invest in on his own. Buying stocks out there is an invitation to a nightmare.

So when it comes to international investing, a mutual fund can be of enormous value. The best mutual fund companies have people who grew up in Japan and Germany and Brazil. They know the cultures as well as the economies. They read reports from abroad two weeks earlier than those dependent on translations. Then the fund sponsors spend big money constantly shipping their people around the world to talk to local brokers and meet with companies.

We need intelligence from abroad when we invest in many U.S companies as well these days, for you can no longer avoid thinking about the world when you look at home industries. A company's competitors can be based anywhere. When the Soviet Union and the Eastern European bloc decommunized, we saw a demand developing for printing presses and packaging materials. Acorn bought Krones (a German firm) and Nordson (a U.S. company)—both makers of packaging and labeling machines—and Komori Printing Machinery (Japan). Making out well with U.S. cellular phone stocks led us to Securicor, a U.K. company; and the success of Wace, an electronic typesetting company in the United Kingdom, told us to look at a similar U.S. company, Devon Group. That's the way it often is these days.

Vanity, No Bonfire

Every public company must have a stock symbol, of no more than four letters. Since there is an unlimited supply of companies to take public, but only a limited number of four-letter codes, the investment banking profession has had to deal with a major challenge.

We can quickly illuminate the critical nature of the ticker-symbol shortage by focusing on the laser industry. Many start-up companies have used laser technology, so the ticker symbols in use include

LASR	LASX
LASE	LSR
LAZR	LSER

There aren't many other ways to almost spell "laser." The next wave of laser companies kept the *L*—LPAC, LMTS, LSCP, and LSRI—but didn't sound very lasery. A linguistic breakthrough was required, and American ingenuity succeeded! Summit Technology found BEAM, and Helionetics coined the immortal ZAP.

Many ticker symbols are simply the equivalent of vanity license plates. They are abbreviations of the name or the initials of the company: OAK for Oak Industries, MAN for Manpower, IGT for International Game Technology. Some are more ingenious: BSMT for Filene's Basement and RAZR for American Safety Razor. Entrepreneurs often use their first names to create vanity tickers: ELY for Callaway Golf, CARL for Karcher Enterprises.

Then we move from prose to poetry. These ticker symbols refer to the company's line of business, but metaphorically.

ROCK	Gibraltar Steel
ZEUS	Olympic Steel
LODE	Comstock Bank
HAMS	Smithfield Companies
JAVA	Mr. Coffee
RARE	Bugaboo Creek Steak House
NOSH	Kineret Acquisition (now Hain Food)
FOTO	Seattle Filmworks
FON	Sprint Corporation
BLUD	Immucor
BID	Sotheby's
DOSE	Choice Drug Systems

Two special favorites of mine:

GAIT	Langer Biomechanics, a researcher into foot and limb biomechanics
BAK	Clinicorp, an owner of chiropractic centers

One level of sophistication yet remains. Here you need inside information to decode the name. FISH, for example, represents Small's Oilfield Services; the company rents oil tools that *fish* for junk stuck in the drill pipe. CHAI is Hebrew for "life," now the toast of Life Medical Services. Exide Electronics makes uninterruptible power supply units, so its ticker is XUPS.

Cute can get too cute. Glacier Water couldn't use WATR (Tetra-Tech has it), so they tried for H2O. They adopted HOO. Nice try, bad chemistry.

Hot Hands, Cool Heads

There's another aspect to professionalism. A professional must try to keep emotion out of what he does. Emotion is marvelous in poetry or on TV or in the bedroom, but you don't particularly want it in high-risk situations. You don't want to fly behind an emotional airline pilot, you don't want to be operated on by an emotional cardiac surgeon. You want someone who stays cool, especially when the unexpected happens.

I don't claim professional portfolio managers are immune to emotional responses to five-hundred-point drops in the Dow Industrials or don't get attached to favorite stocks, but I do believe they are more objective than most individual investors. They are less likely to panic in bear markets and more likely to be skeptical in boom times. On the whole, they are readier to admit mistakes and take losses. They are inundated daily with contrary views, which fosters objectivity. They are, in short, more rational when tough decisions have to be made. Also, they understand the seriousness of their responsibility for other people's money and take pride, therefore, in acting professionally. True, their own money is usually at risk, too, for most mutual fund managers have a good chunk of their personal net worth mixed in the pot with yours, but that adds motivation without taking away from the realization that the overwhelming percentage of the fund represents other people's life savings.

All things considered, then, mutual funds make sense for most people. I can see what legendary former Fidelity Magellan manager Peter Lynch was driving at—though I suspect he was indulging in a bit of hyperbole—when he wrote: "Twenty years in this business convinces me that any normal person using the customary three percent of the brain can pick stocks just as well as, if not better than, the average Wall Street expert." Maybe Lynch knew my Uncle David. But there's more to managing a pile of money than picking stocks. There's tracking their progress, knowing when they should be sold, getting the right mix of stocks, adding the garlic and lemongrass of foreign issues, and all the rest. It is not a job for amateurs who aren't willing to commit a great deal of time and study to the process.

Nor am I impressed by the studies that show that the average professional investor doesn't beat "the market," usually referring to the Standard & Poor's 500 Index. After all, professional investors run some 90 percent of the market. By definition, a huge group cannot beat its own average, for the same reason you can't bite your own ear.

An index fund provides average performance at a fraction of the cost of an actively managed fund, and over time that cost advantage accumulates and gradually raises the index fund in the rankings of all funds. The average manager should generate the results of the index minus 1 percent expenses, which is exactly what the statistics show. Garrison Keillor described the village of Lake Wobegon as the place where "all the children are above average." Professional money managers can't make that claim.

An index fund does have its advantages: *(a)* you know you will get good long-term performance, because stocks return more than bonds or cash, and *(b)* you can have confidence in advance that it will be good long-term performance. That's really valuable. A fund manager can tell you that his company has a great system, great people, great everything, and that performance over the next ten years is going to be sensational. But his enthusiasm may prove nothing more than marketing hyperbole, and you'll end up with below-average performance. With an index fund, you don't have to worry about that.

When you decide on active management instead of an index fund, you are putting your faith in a manager, a philosophy, a method, and a long-term record. You are saying, "What I know of this person gives me reasonable assurance that I will get something better than average performance over time, with very little danger of really bad performance."

That seems to me a rational risk to take. There is no kind of work that I can think of where some people aren't better than average at what they do. The long-term records of fund managers are there to study: go for the best. When it comes to mutual funds, the best usually costs no more.

There is still one other reason to invest through mutual funds rather than on your own. It gives you someone to blame if there's a screw-up.

In any case, I would be willing to bet my Boy Scout merit badges that even the average professional manager beats the average individual investor. I know the stupid things we professionals do, but they are almost surely less stupid than the things the typical citizen does on his own.

There is still one other reason to invest through mutual funds rather than on your own. It gives you someone to blame if there's a screw-up or the market takes a prolonged dive. "Gee, honey," you can explain to your spouse when you inform him or her that the money to refurbish the family room just isn't there this year, "it wasn't my fault. I know I'm no expert, so I went to the professionals. It was that damn fool in Chicago who lost our money, not me."

Picking One from Column B

How do you pick a good mutual fund? I've always had a ready answer: "Alphabetically."

The number of funds that have come into being in the last few years is staggering. At least it has staggered me. There has to be some kind of limit to this growth. I've decided it's the point at which there is one fund per capita. When we reach the day when there are more mutual funds than there are people, then the growth rate will start to slow down.

There is such extensive coverage of mutual funds today, in half a dozen magazines and from various services, that I can't believe you need my help in identifying the good ones. Or at least in eliminating the bad ones. Most of the rankings and grading systems are based on performance, and though past good performance is no guarantee of future good performance, you probably don't want to pick a fund with an absolutely god-awful ten-year record.

But as for the leaders in the rankings, knowing what a fund did last year or the last three years (and you'd better make sure the manager who created those numbers is still in charge) gives you only a meager indication of what it's likely to do in the next year or three years. You have to send for the prospectus of any fund that interests you and really read it, along with any other literature included in the package. You want to find out what the fund's operating philosophy is. If you can't figure it out—maybe the manager doesn't even have one—throw the material in the wastebasket. If a philosophy is spelled out, then you must decide if it appeals to you, if it looks as if the manager operates in a way you think makes sense, probably the way you'd go about it yourself if you had the time and resources. You can't predict how a fund is going to perform in the next year or two, but you will rest easier, whatever happens, if you have confidence in the way you know the manager is handling your money.

Some people want a fifty-five-year-old manager with a wealth of experience, and others like the idea of a thirty-year-old with fresh ideas and boundless energy. Some investors don't mind a high-turnover fund, figuring the manager is an aggressive opportunist; others are turned off by constant trading. Some can feel comfortable only with a blue chip orientation, while others are drawn to funds loaded with exciting telecommunications and software companies. But if the fund is heavily invested in high-multiple high-tech, you have to understand that there's a good possibility that when the market's down 5 percent, your fund will drop 20 percent. If you can't stand that kind of volatility, you won't be happy even when your fund is making money, because you'll be worried all the time.

You have to own what makes you comfortable, but you also have to diversify. If you know you are value oriented—the kind of person who shops at Filene's Basement instead of Neiman Marcus—by all means choose value managers, one for large-cap and one for small-cap stocks. But then put some money into a growth stock fund as well. As we saw in an earlier chapter, value and growth managers have alternative days in the sun, and you should have a claim on the fortunes of both styles. And you should have some exposure—at least 20 percent—in international funds. I'll have more to say on that topic in a later chapter.

I'm a believer in no-load funds, by the way, and not just because my funds are no-loads. Most obviously, a no-load fund delivers a more economically effective package. All of the customer's money goes into investments instead of Mercedes-Benzes for salesmen.

But beyond that, the no-load investor has to do his or her own research rather than rely on a broker, and that's a healthy exercise. Someone who has gone to the trouble of collecting and studying prospectuses and then made a careful decision about which funds to be in has convinced himself of the rightness of those funds for himself. He then has a vested interest in his decision and tends to be loyal to the funds he's chosen. He doesn't keep switching funds on the advice of some newsletter guru, so that he's always backing last year's winner. And he's more likely to stay with his manager when the market sours instead of jumping into a money market fund and then missing half of the market's rebound.

Because the no-load fund investor does his own research rather than relying on a broker, he's more likely to retain confidence in his funds when the market turns nasty.

The truth of the matter is, mutual fund shareholders aren't as performance conscious as one would think looking at the endless rankings in the press. Your average investor doesn't spend his Sunday afternoons comparing his fund's performance to the S&P 500, and doesn't really care whether his fund ranked sixth or eleventh or twenty-second last month, and isn't upset because he might have squeezed out another 3 percent if he'd been in Fund X instead of Fund Y. He figures Fund X simply took more risk. He's done his research, he trusts his manager, and he knows for sure that manager is going to do better running a portfolio than he would himself. So he's content.

The performance derby, I've found, with all the hoopla it generates, is more important to fund managers than it is to the rank-and-file investor. Fund management is a viciously competitive game, with the score posted daily. Which means a manager never has an easy year, even in bull markets, because if you're up 52 percent, somebody else is going to be up 53 percent, and you're still in second place.

Outside of professional athletes, it's hard to think of any other group that has to put up with as much statistical measurement in their lives. Lawyers, doctors, journalists, and other professionals don't have to face this constant, precise weighing of performance. Accountants don't go around proclaiming, "You know, of course, that I rank sixteenth of the two hundred and seventy-one accountants in this city." A professor isn't going to get a phone call from somebody who says, "Hey, last year you were the thirteenth-best English literature teacher in the United States and this year you slipped to eighteenth. What do you think is your problem?"

There's little evidence that the manager whose performance has been far above average over the last three years is going to maintain that record over the coming three years.

I suppose all this measuring is to be expected. Newspapers and magazines run tables of relative performance because performance is the only thing they can measure. If your only tool is a hammer, every problem looks like a nail. If you're trying to make a living commenting on mutual funds, what else is there to comment on?

Loyalty to a manager you trust is critical, because no one can give you top-of-the-heap performance year after year. In fact, one thing you can be certain of when it comes to performance is that it's not going to be the same next year. Guys who have done a terrible job over the last ten years, it is true, tend to keep doing a terrible job. But there's not much evidence that the manager who has been far above average over the last three or five years is going to maintain that record over the coming three or five years. The evidence shows, in fact, that people tend to drop back. Reversion to the mean is a powerful force, and we'll have more to say about it later.

All you can do is try to find somebody whose long-term record, with all the great and not-so-great years, is better than that of the fund's market sector and the average fund in its group, and whose style you have confidence in because it matches the way you think about risk and the market. And once you've found that person, as long as your confidence holds, stick with him or her.

6

THEMES AND VARIATIONS

Artur Rubinstein, the great pianist, who died in 1982, was once asked to judge a piano competition in London. The scorecards were to be marked on a scale of one to twenty, the most gifted to receive the highest number. Rubinstein listened intently to the students' recitals and marked his cards as each finished. When the sponsors of the competition examined the scores at the end of the competition they were astonished to see that most of the players had been given zeros and a few, twenties; there were no intermediate scores. The sponsors hurried to the great master and demanded to know why he had judged the entrants in such an arbitrary manner.

"Simple enough," replied the virtuoso. "Either they can play the piano or they cannot."

The Rubinstein Rule is critically important to my approach to the stock market. Rather than build a broadly diversified stock portfolio, I believe in determining themes I think will be played out over the next several years and then identifying groups of stocks that reflect those themes. My portfolio may own a considerable number of stocks, but most of them by far will fall into a half-dozen or fewer themes. The Rubinstein Rule dictates that either a stock group is worth playing or it is not worth considering at all.

Yes, my search for themes means that I am not a pure "stock picker," looking for "great stocks" wherever I can find them. Of course, I want the most attractive stocks that reflect the themes, but the themes come first.

First I determine themes that will be played out over the next several years. Then I identify groups of stocks that reflect those themes.

Perhaps this will disappoint the reader. Stock pickers have become celebrities, the Rubinsteins of the investment world, the reputed possessors of an uncanny skill in uncovering gems hidden from the eyes of ordinary mortals. In practical terms, however, there are some ten thousand publicly traded companies out there, which makes for a lot of haystacks in which to hunt for needles. I think it makes sense to narrow the search.

I am reminded of the old plate spinner act you used to see on television variety programs. The spinner puts a thin rod into a socket resting on the floor, places a dinner plate atop the rod, and pumps the rod vigorously until the plate is spinning fast enough to stay on top of the rod unaided. After plate one has stabilized (working as a simple gyroscope), the spinner sets up another rod with another plate on it. Soon plate number two is spinning alongside number one. Number three sets up easily, then number four—but now number one is wobbling dangerously and needs cranking up again. The spinner keeps adding plates—a dozen or more—just managing to rescue the one about to fall and shatter on the floor. As the act builds toward its climax, the spinner is running from plate to plate faster and faster, cranking desperately, until everyone in the audience is laughing uncontrollably.

Everyone, that is, except the mutual fund portfolio managers watching. They are reminded, painfully, of every day at the office. Trying to keep current on fifty or a hundred and fifty stocks in a mutual fund, while studying new ones, can be a plate-spinning nightmare. The manager is forever hastening from crisis to crisis, with some position always on the edge of a crash, with results that may be anything but hilarious for the fund shareholders.

Funds do well only so long as portfolio decisions are made by a small group of people.

Every stock in a portfolio is a spinning plate, cranked up with security analysis instead of energy. Since this analytic work must factor in political, economic, and market variables as well as corporate developments, keeping all one's stocks in the air at once is a prodigious job. And the world is crueler than is evident, for portfolio management theory demands that the risks and rewards of each stock be constantly compared with those of every other stock, both those within the portfolio and all other possibilities. The truth is, it can't be done: no organization, no matter how large, can keep that many plates spinning. At Acorn, for example, we could hire a very large staff of analysts to cover more companies, but large organizations usually haven't had very good results as fund managers. Superior analysts are rare, and funds seem to do well only so long as the decisions are made by a small group of talented people.

The bottom-up stock picker, who selects his stocks one by one, ending up with the one hundred best picks regardless of industry or risk classification, must feel like the ultimate plate spinner. I prefer the greater control and the selectivity of a "top-down" portfolio management philosophy. I look for areas of the market that seem to me particularly compelling, thus reducing the analytic process to the selection of a few attractive stocks from each identified group.

The individual investor, admittedly, doesn't have to juggle hundreds of stocks. He can just pick off the dozen or so he is drawn to. But in selecting the stocks he hopes will double or triple over time—the short-term trader is playing in a different ballpark—he'll improve his chances of success if he finds companies operating in a favorable environment.

Trend Spotting

The market areas and the groups I want to concentrate on are those that I believe will benefit from strong economic, social, or technological trends.

Furthermore, I want to identify trends that will last four or five years or longer, thus putting my investment horizon beyond the next business cycle or some analyst's estimate of next year's earnings. I also escape the shackles of the efficient-market hypothesis, which states that earnings and prospects for the next quarter and year are already reflected in the market price of a stock, for I am looking beyond the next quarter and year.

> I concentrate on areas that will benefit from strong economic, social, or technological trends. And I want trends that will last four years or longer.

As I discussed earlier, the institutionalization of the market, with managers like myself all fed the same information on-line, has made it harder and harder to find undervalued stocks. The overcrowding of professional investors into the one-to-two-year fore-casting horizon makes any consistent superiority of results in this time slot improbable. One solution, we've seen, is to buy smaller companies most institutions are not interested in. Another (and compatible) response is to look beyond the next quarter and the next year and search, instead, for very-long-term trends.

What I am trying to avoid is what I call the "forecasting horizon trap." From the point of view of a sound long-term investor, most security analysts' reports are mere journalism, not analysis. But be-cause analysts spend so much time pumping corporate managers for information—about sales trends, price changes, and costs—their short-term earnings forecasts are generally reliable. A typical cor-porate president working in April 1997 may have finally under-stood what happened in 1996 and the first quarter of 1997. The second quarter of 1997 being in progress, he can probably make a well-informed estimate about its results.

But the second half of the year? "Well, that will be affected by trends in the economy that aren't certain, but assuming that busi-ness gets better than it was in the first half . . ." Estimates for 1998 are based on even more tenuous assumptions. For more than cigh-teen months out, 1999 and into the next millennium, analysts tend merely to extend past trend lines. "Beefsteak Mines has had sales growth averaging 11 percent a year for ten years, so let's assume sales in 1999 will be up 11 percent from our 1998 estimate." As John Maynard Keynes noted back in 1936, "Our knowledge of the factors which will govern the yield of an investment some years hence is usually very slight and often negligible."

The forecasting horizon trap lures you into spending all your time on what's more knowable—the same immediate horizon that occupies everyone else. If you fall into the trap, competing with all the other investors concentrating on these short-term events, it is impossible to outperform the market, after paying transaction costs. You have to escape to a longer-term perspective.

Remember, too, what I said in Chapter 2 about small-company

stocks in particular. Over the long run, well-selected small companies will do better than large companies because the smaller ones haven't exhausted most of their growth potential. But trading small-company stocks is difficult. They are often illiquid, and trading costs can be very high. Trying to sell even a modest-size position (the individual investor with a few hundred shares wouldn't have this problem) can knock the price down considerably. The solution to high trading costs is to buy stocks you can hold for a long time.

And again, if you want to keep stocks for years, you can't focus on companies you think are going to have a great quarter. They may have a great quarter and then tread water or go into a slump. If a company reports 28 cents per share for the quarter, beating the Merrill Lynch analyst's forecast by 2 cents, that doesn't excite me. I need a long-term reason to own a stock. I want to see something that convinces me not only that the company's management is competent and its product line exciting but, in addition, that its particular industry, or niche in an industry, is one with superb prospects. I want everything going for me.

If a company's earnings beat the Merrill Lynch analyst's forecast by 2 cents, that doesn't excite me. I need a long-term reason to own a stock.

In choosing companies, however, I can't make specific forecasts about 1998 earnings any better than anyone else can. But I can invest in a stock with far greater confidence if I believe it will benefit from a major trend that I have identified, a thematic concept about the world that will hold true for a number of years to come.

Often, of course, you are looking for the leaders in the industry you believe is nicely positioned, like International Game Technology in a world gone mad for gambling. But at other times it's not necessarily the industry leaders that will benefit most from a trend. For example, if you think energy prices are going to rise, you probably want to own oil producers; but if you think energy prices are likely to fall, you should invest in companies that are heavy users of energy, like the airlines, or will benefit from its cheapness, like hotels, resorts, and recreational vehicles. You have to think through whose earnings should get the biggest boost. In a gold rush it's not the miners who get rich but those who sell the prospectors their pants.

An Unclouded Crystal Ball

How does one identify investment themes? As Sherlock Holmes, with his usual maddening superiority, chastised Watson, "You see but you do not observe." The investor has to develop an observing mind-set and get in the habit of looking for trends in his reading and experience. Perhaps a newspaper account of what's going on in the job market will suggest a thriving area of the economy that can lead to an investment opportunity. Thinking about the fact that so many of the fastest-growing cities—Phoenix, Las Vegas, Palm Springs—are built in deserts, I began to wonder what they do for water, which led me to invest in Western Water, a company that had been thinking along the same lines. You might spot a trend developing in your own line of work, or pick up something from trade journals, which usually report on trends before they make the newspapers. Driving around town and seeing the number of cars parked in front of Toys "R" Us might have alerted you to watch out for the next superstores, so that you made a lot of money in Home Depot, Staples, Sports Authority, and Borders. You have to train yourself to make generalizations from random particulars, to keep asking yourself, "What does this mean?"

Sometimes the themes are staring you in the face. A number of years ago Barton Biggs, now chairman of Morgan Stanley Asset Management, published a short story about a man who was supernaturally provided with tomorrow's *Wall Street Journal* and thus easily made his way to a fortune. I think at times that is precisely what we can do. Some things we know are going to happen, and we can use that knowledge to make a lot of money. Let me show you how to read next year's newspaper.

We know with certainty that underdeveloped countries will invest in telephone systems.

In the United States there are about seventy telephones for every hundred people. In Japan and many parts of Europe the number is relatively the same. Go to poorer countries like Mexico, Russia, Brazil, and Egypt, and the number comes way down. In China, near the bottom of the curve, there's seven-tenths of a telephone for every hundred people. We have one hundred times more telephones per capita than the Chinese. We *know* everyone wants more telephones. The Chinese like to talk just as much as Americans do. We also *know* from governmental pronouncements and contracts being signed that it is going to happen. China's announced that it wants to build 10 million phone lines over the next ten years, which would bring the country from seven-tenths of a phone per one hundred persons to seven phones per one hundred, about where Mexico and Malaysia are now. And of course by that time Mexico and Malaysia will have moved well up the curve.

The expansion of telephone systems is probably a theme you are already familiar with. There are now several mutual funds dedicated to that very thesis. But you could have identified this theme several years ago and made many times your money—the run-up in Teléfonos de México being the best known example.

But that development thesis can be extended beyond phone lines. In all these emerging economies a middle class will evolve, and in frontier economies changes can happen remarkably quickly. Discretionary spending can easily grow at a 10-to-20-percent annual rate for many years. The growth of a middle class in developing countries is a very simple but powerful way to think about the future. First the newly well-off want bicycles, then motorcycles, and, five years from now, automobiles.

Another change that occurs when you become middle class is that you start to take vacations. Especially in countries that are small and overcrowded and whose population is homogeneous, there's a great desire to see different lands. The emerging middle class will travel to Australia or Hawaii or Switzerland or Bali to experience a different climate and see different people and sights. Translating that wanderlust into investments, our analysts have invested in the stocks of Genting International (a Singapore cruise line), H.I.S. (a Japanese travel agency), and Burswood (an Australian casino).

The growth of a middle class in developing countries is a very simple—but powerful—way to think about the future. First the newly well-off want bicycles, then motorcycles, and five years from now, automobiles.

Some of the upwardly mobile middle class climb into the upper class. There are already tens of thousands of very wealthy entrepreneurs in these countries, and they love luxury status symbols from the West—Tiffany jewelry, Escada suits, BMWs. These are all supplied by publicly owned companies.

Mistakenly Identified

Of course, not all long-term themes are as certain bets as the spread of phone systems. Some of my most carefully considered forecasts have proved dead wrong. Around 1980 I thought we were going to run out of oil and gas, which the Iran-Iraq war seemed to confirm. (In surmising how Mideast nations would line up behind these adversaries, I noted that "Politics make strange Bedouin fellows.") A lot of people thought the same, and we were all wrong. I should have bailed out of the oil stocks instead of increasing my position right at the top. It created a bit of a disaster for a time.

In 1984, looking at industry's ever-growing reliance on information technology, I joked to an interviewer that IBM would continue to grow 12 to 15 percent a year until "it'll overtake everything; pretty soon the U.S. government will be known as IBM's North American division." The joke had a point. IBM proved once again that very high growth rates cannot last forever.

What Can We Say About the Future?

Trying to discern current or nascent trends with some staying power is not the same as crystal-balling the far-off future. The future is always full of surprises. Go back twenty-five years and nobody worried about smoking cigarettes. The idea of getting up early to go jogging would have seemed absurd. If it had been clear what was developing, medical school students could have switched from cardiology to sports medicine. But technology has not yet produced a time machine.

Occasionally, I am asked to give a talk before a group, and when it's a general audience rather than a herd of investment people, I know I am going to be asked, "Ralph, where do you think the market's headed?" (Investment professionals aren't likely to bother, knowing my guess is no better than theirs.) In January 1990 I gave a speech to the Rotary Club in Chicago, aware that I would be expected to predict what the market would do not only that year but in the coming decade. I forestalled that request by asking my audience to think back to January 1980 and ask themselves what they thought the eighties would bring. How many of us would have thought that

1. The U.S. economy would provide seven consecutive years without a recession, the longest stretch, up to that time, in peacetime history;

2. The Soviet bloc in Eastern Europe would revolt against communism and Soviet domination, and the U.S.S.R. would not intervene;

3. A new major disease would torment us (AIDS wasn't known to exist in 1980);

4. The price of oil would drop in half (Everyone in 1980 expected the price of a barrel of oil in 1990 would be nearing $100);

5. The United States would go from being the largest creditor nation in the world, in 1980, to the largest debtor nation.

That is why, I told my listeners, I had no intention of making predictions about the 1990s. And I'm glad I kept my mouth shut. I was certainly not someone who foresaw the imminent collapse of communism not only in Eastern Europe but in the Soviet Union itself. As for the stock market, practically no one in my business expected one of the greatest bull markets in history was about to begin—not after the already generous returns of the eighties.

Even predicting the effects of known technologies is difficult. This was made embarrassingly clear when the MIT journal *Technology Review* published an article in 1983 called "Disagreeing with the Future," which examined a set of predictions made by "professional futurists" in 1972 about what life would be like in 1980–85. All of the twenty items forecast seemed like good prospects in 1972; they were made by sensible, well-trained people, and they predicated projects that were socially beneficial and that used technology for the most part already invented. It was predicted, for example, that no cars would be allowed in most downtown areas, and that business travel and mail would be *down* 25 percent as people relied on audiovisual communication. Most of the other forecasts were equally wrong.

Just as important were the forecasts the futurists *didn't* make. There were no forecasts about personal computers, microwave ovens, cellular phones, video recorders, or extended-wear contact lenses.

Admitting the occasional miscalculations, I think one *can* nevertheless identify economic, social, and technological trends that will be important for the next several years, and decide when those trends have waned. It is certainly easier to do than it is to forecast where the market itself is headed, and more sensible. The market may be strong or weak, and the stocks that I choose as beneficiaries of trends may for a while be strong or weak in consequence, but if I am right in my themes, I know that in time my stocks will do fine and I needn't worry as much about the market's ups and down.

Recognizing the fallibility of almost any forecast, including my own, here are the investment themes we are working with in 1996 that should have several years of life left in them.

THE REBUILDING OF A CRUMBLING GLOBAL INFRASTRUCTURE

Business activity has been growing rapidly in a newly free-market-oriented world, but the systems that support it have not kept pace. The world needs more electric power plants, highways, bridges, airports, communications systems, and pollution controls. Stocks of engineering, construction, and equipment companies are the obvious choice. Terry Hogan in our offices found Thermo Electron, which makes products that reduce pollution and modernize plants, and AES China Generating, a U.S. company building electrical generating plants in China.

THE EXPANSION OF WORLD COMMUNICATIONS NETWORKS

A company can now have a branch in Sri Lanka and manage it almost as efficiently as if it were in Atlanta. Cheap, fast communications and transportation have created the globalization you are probably sick of hearing about, but it's all true and can only continue. Expeditors, an airfreight forwarding company, has been a great investment.

THE BUSINESS OF LEISURE

America leads the world in leisure. Maybe we don't work as hard as the Japanese and aren't as thrifty as the Swiss, but we party great. Disney could not have been invented in any other country. Fun is a very serious business.

I've owned broadcasting, movie chain, and shopping center stocks, but the one that's been a key position for some time has been Carnival Corporation. The cruise vacations it offers are very appealing: Your decisions are made for you and your costs are controlled. You are not going to get eaten by a lion or catch cholera. There's lots of food and you can boogie all night. Carnival has the leading market share in the vacation-cruise business, the most professional management, the highest margins, the most modern ships, the best advertising and marketing to the economy end of the cruise market, and the best relationships with travel agents. Its earnings have been growing 20 percent a year, and will continue to excel, especially if Castro finally packs it in. Cuba's an ideal destination for folks cruising out of Miami.

Collecting the Wages of Sin

In a society determined to have a good time in its leisure hours, with airports, resorts, restaurants, and gambling casinos all doing fine, it would seem that hedonism is triumphant. But public moods go through cycles, the oldest of all cycles—from good to bad and back to good again.

In the 1960s, the good was ascendant. We refer to the altruistic and idealistic sentiments that prevailed then: pacifism, ecology, integration, and antimaterialism. Tens of billions of dollars were allocated to urban renewal, clean air and water, education and training for minorities, worker safety, and other worthy endeavors. I owned a number of stocks of companies that seemed essential to these initiatives.

Then, in the late seventies and the Reagan eighties, the pendulum swung back. As the hippies matured and entered the workforce, they found they wanted to keep their money for themselves instead of paying more taxes. The perfectibility of man and society was now perceived as an illusion anyway, so let the less fortunate of the world save themselves instead of our having to do it. So badness came in.

At one point, to prove that badness was more profitable than goodness in the emerging environment, we tested two portfolios, one of which exuded sanctity, while the other oozed vice. Vice won, and about time, too, because there's more profit in it.

36-MONTH PRICE CHANGE
September 30, 1975–September 30, 1978

VIRTUOUS PORTFOLIO		WICKED PORTFOLIO	
Angelica	+45%	Playboy	+600%
L. S. Good	+5%	Frederick's of	
Church's Fried		Hollywood	23%
Chicken	+520%	Golden Nugget	+197%
Mangood Ind.	+30%	National Distillers	+45%
St. Joseph Light	+29%	U.S. Tobacco	+87%
Friendly Ice Cream	−29%	DeBeers Mines	+59%
Average	+100%	Average	+161%

The prime test of my theory was the superstock of the year, which went nowhere when it had the "good" name of Mary Carter Paint, but which went from less than $1 to a high of $70 after it changed its name to Resorts International.

Statistical Note: This study was done by the usual techniques of financial analysis: *(a)* the stocks chosen have nothing to do with the subject and *(b)* the portfolios were readjusted until the answer affirmed the hypothesis. A superior methodology would have been: (1) select more representative sample portfolios and (2) if the results contradict the hypothesis, ignore the results. A good theory can withstand mere disproof.

ENERGY EXPLORATION

The major oil companies—Texaco, Amoco, Arco, and the other O's—are going offshore. They think the United States has been drilled up. They don't see any places worth exploring, except maybe the middle of the Gulf of Mexico or Alaska. They are probably right: there are few large pools of oil still to be found in the continental United States. So the majors have been having a kind of clearance sale. At the same time, a number of independents are giving up on the business. They're too small, business is too scuzzy, so they're cashing it in. Old Billy Bob wants out; he's seventy-two, and the hell with this stuff.

Enter the jackal companies, which pick up these properties on the cheap and then are often able to improve them—shoot some new seismic, redrill some wells, put in a new gathering system or new compressors or whatever's needed. They can make a nice business out of these old, marginal fields. Acorn has bought several of these so-called exploitation companies—Benton Oil & Gas, Basin Exploration, and Snyder Oil Corp., all fairly small companies. A slightly larger one that has also performed well for us is Seagull Energy.

THE LIBERALIZATION OF EASTERN EUROPE

Russia and the former Soviet satellites need just about everything on their journey to capitalism. I've mentioned that I've owned printing press and packaging machinery companies, Nordson, Komori, and Krones. Another crying need of the old Iron Curtain countries is the equipment made by Mine Safety Appliances, a U.S. company with production facilities in Germany. It is the world's largest manufacturer of industrial safety equipment—everything from goggles and hard-toe shoes to masks, respirators, and sophisticated analytic equipment—all materials that Eastern Europe badly needs.

NATIONALISM

Like it or not, nationalism is a stronger force than ever. Everyone wants his own country. There's been an explosion in country names. A mapmaker would be a good investment, but Rand McNally is virtually a private company. The third thing you do when you start a new country is print your own money. (The first thing you do is design a flag. The second is get your mistress a bigger apartment.) So I own Stevens International, which has a license to print money. Our own Bureau of Engraving and Printing is a customer. The French government is another.

OUTSOURCING

Many businesses—abroad as well as in this country—have been deciding that they can be more efficient, effective, and competitive if they buy certain services on the outside that they have heretofore taken care of internally. Temporary-help companies are an early example, and Manpower has been one of our rewarding investments. Today, there are service companies that will take on total office assignments. Systems and Computer Technology runs the business offices of universities. Capita, an English company, manages the driver's license offices of some municipalities. Serco, another U.K. company, runs prisons, RAF bases, and research laboratories.

But outsourcing is now expanding beyond administrative services. Steel mills, for example, are increasingly concentrating solely on manufacturing, letting somebody else do the processing, warehousing, and distribution. And steel users are doing the same, hiring outsiders for fabrication assignments. Instead of shipping a coil of steel, for example, Worthington Industries will, if requested, stamp disks out of the coils and ship the disks instead. Worthington, blessed with superior management and excelling at both customer service and employee relations, has been a great stock.

I think the outsourcing theme is going to be lucrative for a long time. Industry will increasingly rely on companies that can concentrate on the technologies and skilled personnel needed to do specialized jobs.

MONEY MANAGEMENT

Most governments in the Western world have made promises to their people that they will be taken care of. In the United States those promises have been carried out in programs such as Social Security, Medicare, and Medicaid. Other countries have similar programs under various names.

These programs have worked as a kind of Ponzi scheme. The people who thought up Social Security in the first place knew it was unsound—and probably unconstitutional—but they wanted to do it anyway, because they thought people would like it. And they were correct. For Americans, it was an imported idea. Germany's Bismarck was the first to introduce a socialist insurance scheme. He was also the one who decided on sixty-five as the retirement age. He was very clever, since few people lived to be sixty-five back then. Today, sixty-five is considered middle-aged.

The working population has been taxed to pay the pensions of the retired population, and as long as there were plenty of workers and not too many retired people, the scheme worked well enough. But Ponzi schemes fail after a while because there aren't enough people to supply the new money to keep the game going. This has now happened for governments. Demographics have gone against them: birthrates have declined to the point where there are no longer rapidly expanding workforces, whereas life expectancies have increased, leaving many more retirees drawing their pensions for far more years. The numbers no longer work. The scheme has collapsed.

Governments now realize that if they try to honor their existing promises, they will either have to raise taxes on workers to the point where they will revolt and refuse to pay them, or reduce benefits. For example, retirement rules can be changed to raise the age at which one is entitled to benefits, or cost-of-living indexing can be dropped. The same choices face Canada, Britain, Italy, and much of the world.

But there is another alternative: privatizing the pension scheme. It's happened in Chile. In 1980 the government-run pension system was replaced by a private system of pension savings accounts.*

It's going to happen throughout the West. Early in 1997 a U.S. federal Advisory Council on Social Security suggested that Congress should consider some degree of privatization of the U.S. system. This could be accomplished in a number of ways. Payroll taxes now invested in special Treasury bonds could be invested in stocks and bonds, probably by way of an index fund of some sort. Others on the panel went further: They proposed that some percentage of the tax go into workers' self-directed retirement accounts, the balance left to maintain the existing flat-benefit system, though at a reduced level. The self-directed portion would go into some kind of mutual fund family. It'll take considerable time before all this is worked out, but some form of privatization is almost inevitable.

Meanwhile, people in this country sense the precariousness of today's Social Security. They have gotten the message that the government isn't going to take care of them, so they had better start saving for themselves. The assets in 401(k) and other defined-contribution plans are growing so rapidly that before long they will exceed the assets in traditional pension plans. Most of that money is flowing into mutual funds.

Two stocks we have owned are T. Rowe Price, a public mutual fund company, and United Asset Management, a kind of holding company for money management firms. Seeing the same forces at work in Europe, I've owned several mutual fund companies there. With billions pouring into funds every week in this country, and

*José Piñera, *Empowering Workers: The Privatization of Social Security in Chile* (Washington, D.C.: Cato Institute, 1966).

the possibility that a Social Security overhaul will pump in more billions, the future will bring continued growth for money management companies—a growth that would be very hard to dam up.

All Good Things . . .

How do you know when a theme is played out? Usually it starts to become obvious: prices have gone too high, Wall Street is cranking out new issues to fit the fashion, magazine cover stories are declaring its importance.

Sometimes the clues are more subtle. Little items can be telling. Scholars puzzling over the identity of the author of an anonymous manuscript often find it less useful to examine thoughts, characters, and sentence structure than (as an example of purposeful nitpicking) to simply count the number of times the author wrote "that" rather than "which," or "shall" instead of "will." The classic example in my own experience of reading the fine print to discern the end of an investment trend occurred in July 1983, when a four-inch story in the middle of *The Wall Street Journal* caught my eye.

> SAN ANTONIO, Texas—Petroleum Acreage Corp. of Texas said it is entering the personal-computer business with a $6 million project to make and market computers.
>
> The oil and natural gas exploration and production company said it is arranging financing for the project and plans to form an 80%-owned subsidiary, Pact Computers, Inc. The company said the computer it plans to develop will sell for less than $3,500 and be ready for marketing by the end of 1983. The computer will be able to use software currently available for use on most of the leading personal computers, Petroleum Acreage said.
>
> A company spokesman said that computer operations could become a major part of the company's business within two years if the new computer's sales meet expectations.

That sounded a little strange. Why would an oil company decide to go into the computer business? Petroleum Acreage Corp. was selling that day at 19/32 bid, it turned out, not a typical price for a classy company. A look in our reference material disclosed that Petroleum Acreage had been in business for less than three years, having gone public in April 1981 at $1 a share. The company had incorporated on November 5, 1980. That was an interesting date—within thirty days of the end of the 1980 superboom in oil stocks! Here was a company formed to exploit one stock market boom, coming to market near the top for the energy stocks, now switching into another hot-stock industry, personal computers.

If you can see where the con men are flocking, you can tell which groups are about to peak.

I considered that announcement a clear warning that personal computer stocks were near their high. We sold some of our holdings and should have dumped more. If you had bought a representative package of microcomputer stocks on July 25, the day that Petroleum Acreage Corp. of Texas announced its entry into the field, by the end of the year you would have lost about a third of your money. If you can see where the con men are flocking, you can tell which groups have become too popular and are probably about to peak.

Niche Knacks

Do I ever buy a stock just because I like the company and the stock's price, even if no theme is evident? Sure. I'm not going to turn away any good situation. But I have a guideline for those stocks, too: I want the company to have a near monopoly in some market niche, or a special quality that makes me believe it is going to be successful for a long time. The company has a franchise, and that franchise is a kind of theme in itself. Then I know, until the company's special position is challenged, that I have a long-term holding. On time horizons I will not compromise.

Do I ever buy a stock even if no theme is evident? Sure. But only if the company has a monopoly or near monopoly on some market niche.

The cellular phone business in a given area is a prime example, as well as reflecting the communications theme. So is the regional bank that dominates its geographical area. I've made a great deal of money over the years in Mine Safety Appliances, the country's biggest industrial safety equipment maker, which also fits into the Eastern European theme. A counterexample was the Canadian company FPI Limited, which had exclusive cod-fishing rights on the Grand Banks, once one of the best fishing holes in the world. But overfishing depleted the codfish population and nixed my fish niche.

Perhaps the niche monopolized most successfully can be claimed by motorcycle maker Harley-Davidson. The whole world has been moving toward a Harley ride. It's the only motorcycle manufacturer in the United States, and the ones outside the United States aren't that exciting. In fact, it just might be the world's best brand name. Coca-Cola is a great brand name, but people don't tattoo it on their body parts.

But my preference is to know that a larger theme is operating— one that gives a stock an edge. And the theme that has been most productive for me deserves its own chapter.

7

DOWNSTREAM FROM TECHNOLOGY

Many years ago, when my daughter Debra was nine years old, I read her the old, comfortable children's book *Mary Poppins*. It's filled with fantastic adventures, but the strangest part of it to me was what the author accepted as plain matter of fact.

The book opens by describing the Banks family as rather ordinary middle class: "Number Seventeen . . . is the smallest house in the lane . . . rather dilapidated and in need of a coat of paint. But Mr. Banks, who owns it, said to Mrs. Banks that she could have either a nice, clean, comfortable house or four children. But not both, for he couldn't afford it."

In this semislum, we find the family faced with a crisis: the nursemaid has quit, and the family is being forced to get by short-handed, with only a cook, a maid, and a houseboy. Luckily, Mary Poppins shows up and allows Mrs. Banks to avoid having to touch her own children.

The time when it took four servants to run an ordinary household seems very far away. Now we have machines instead of house-boys and housegirls. A revolution in energy use has transformed household productivity, transportation, industry, and just about everything else. It would be no exaggeration to say there would have been no Industrial Revolution without the harnessing of cheap carbon, found in coal, oil, and gas. Many of the companies supplying the ever-growing energy needs of our world have proved marvelous investments over most of this century.

But in the last quarter of this century a different theme has emerged. Twenty years ago I wrote that carbon's dominance was being challenged by a second chemical element, silicon. Our ability to place thousands of circuit elements on tiny silicon chips was creating extraordinary information-gathering and -sorting systems. Information processing was become cheaper and cheaper, while energy was rising in price. It was clear, even in the mid-seventies, that "the world will substitute information for energy."

The Information Revolution is the theme I've worked hardest on and that has worked hardest for me. It's a theme that never seems to give out.

That substitution identified a sensational long-term megatrend. Even in 1976 I thought it was kind of old news, but I have continued to invest in that trend ever since. The Information Revolution is the theme I've worked hardest on and that has worked hardest for me. I've practically made a career out of that one idea, since I've consistently built a large part of my portfolios around it. It's a theme that never seems to give out.

Making Schools Human

Spend a day with a ten-year-old boy. You will see him dashing from one activity to the next. Teaching him grammar for forty minutes in an English class is as easy as teaching a hummingbird to play chess. "How was school today, darling?" "Boring!"

Then this kid, this disorganized bundle of nervous energy, will throw down a nourishing dinner of french fries and root beer and disappear upstairs. When you go up to his room two hours later, you find him at his Nintendo helping Mario save a princess. Our hero is engaged, with an industriousness and eagerness that school seldom generates, in learning the rules and strategies of video games, which are much more demanding than any homework assignment. The result is a level of learning far beyond what was attempted in the classroom just a few hours earlier.

I believe computers shouldn't be segregated in a computer lab at schools but should be made available at every student's desk. We have a chance to teach in an effective, lower-cost, and fun way by making the computer in the classroom as much a part of student life as the Sega or Nintendo machine is at home. Computers can do what teachers often cannot: instruct at the individual pupil's level of knowledge, repeat troublesome areas, and keep the student interested through imaginative presentations.

As more educators convert to that point of view, investment opportunities arise. Companies I've owned, such as Sierra On-Line, Software Toolworks, and Electronic Arts, are evolving from video game companies into game-plus-education companies. Jostens and Edunetics go after the school market directly. Sega supplies some of the hardware.

The Users, Not the Makers

I seldom own the companies that develop the new technologies, however—the makers of the computers and the semiconductor chips that go into them. Semiconductors are what really make computers, cellular phones, fax machines, and much else possible. But Motorola and Intel have never been in our portfolio. Intel and Motorola have done well, but other semiconductor makers, such as Fairchild, failed at the game, and anyway, Intel's and Motorola's customers have made more money than they have. New products are dangerous, especially in the computer field, where obsolescence comes fast and technological breakthroughs bring price slashing every year.

What I have always looked for instead are the downstream users of new technologies. I've bought the stocks of companies that buy, use, and exploit the computers and electronics to reduce costs, revitalize their businesses, and add functionality to their products. Even new industries emerge as people figure out ways to use these devices. (And some industries and enterprises can be made obsolete. I believe that the New York Stock Exchange, since we no longer need a hub to create a trading network, is an anachronism that is taking a very long time to die.)

I may never have owned semiconductor companies, but I've

made a considerable amount of money in cellular phone companies—LIN Broadcasting, Mobile Communications, and Telephone &
Data Systems—that use the chips. I didn't buy VCR makers, but I
have owned companies like Electronic Arts and Sierra On-Line,
which make those video games that keep kids away from useful
activities. Television is also dependent on semiconductors, but broadcasting stations have made more profits than the entire semiconductor industry put together. There is no comparing the genius it
requires to run a semiconductor company and the minor talent it
takes to run a television station. But I'm afraid that when you compare profit margins, it just proves the point that in this world the
stupid people can make all the money. Most of the folks running
electronics companies are indeed geniuses, and they've got a building full of even smarter geniuses out back, working like crazy to invent new stuff. But they end up struggling; they have problems in
the competitive world. There's usually some nerd in Austin or
Aoyama who's a little bit ahead of them. The geniuses cancel each
other out. Even if you invent a brand new sixteen-meg chip, you'll
still be surrounded by competitors. But if you have the only channel that can show *Home Improvement* at 7 P.M., you have a monopoly. All you have to do to run a cable company is get a license from
the city and be mean to your customers.

Since the Industrial Revolution began, going downstream—investing in businesses that will benefit from new technology rather
than investing in the technology companies themselves—has often
proved the smarter strategy. The railroad, the product of the transforming technology of the steam locomotive, one of the greatest inventions in history, was obviously of supreme importance to the
United States and its economy. But the makers of the locomotives,
like Baldwin and American Locomotive Works, were not terribly
profitable. The railroads themselves were moderately profitable for
a while, but in the end most of them fared poorly or went broke.
(Their capital came mostly from abroad, an international wealth
transfer, a sort of Marshall Plan in reverse. The savings in English

and Scottish trusts moved over here, and the net return to all those investors was probably zero.)

Going downstream—investing in the businesses that will benefit from new technology rather than in the technology companies themselves—is often the smarter strategy.

Those who really made money out of the new technology were not the transportation people but those who bought real estate in Chicago in the 1880s and 1890s. As the railroad came in and created a city of 3 million people, land values skyrocketed. The railroads that were most successful were those that secured land grants from the government to build the tracks and thus owned some enormously valuable real estate. So the manufacturer who built the steam locomotive made $5, the tycoon who built the railroad made $50, and the land speculator who bought land that later became downtown Wichita made $500.

Similarly, when jet planes—larger and faster than the props—came on the scene, they changed the airline business, but it wasn't the jet-engine makers General Electric, Pratt and Whitney, and Rolls-Royce that benefited most. In that instance it was the airlines that reaped the profits for a while; I know, because—as I mentioned earlier—I did well in airline stocks back then, when the big carriers could actually make money. Now the airline industry is barely breaking even, and airline stocks are only speculations. But think of what the jet plane made possible!

Also in the postwar era, air-conditioning changed the way we all live, but you didn't make much money investing in Carrier and the other makers. But downstream, you could have made a fortune, for air conditioners created the New South. In 1930 the population of

Houston was six men and a dog, and the dog was dead. Houston was in a basically uninhabitable part of the world. But then came air conditioners, which made southern California, Texas, and Arizona boom areas. Phoenix is a thriving city, in spite of the fact that it gets to 116 degrees in the summer. Without air-conditioning it would still be a trading post. So Carrier made a moderate amount of money, but the big money came to the fellows who owned the land, built the tract houses, created the stores (like Phoenix's Goldwater's), and opened the restaurants.

Sometimes it's hard to find a way to play a new technology. The fax machine, for example, has had an enormous impact in business communications, but there is no "fax company," either here or in Japan. Fax machines are just one of the businesses of some large companies. Also, it was a high-risk investment, because it is one of those businesses that can't make money until it's mature. The fax machine existed for at least a decade before it meant anything; the fax machine works only if both you and I have one. Once it reached a critical mass, it exploded. It went from being something you never used into something you use all the time. The laser presents a similar situation. It is a magnificent technology, but there's no such thing as an IBM of the laser industry.

The Mighty Computer

The computer is in a class by itself. It has revolutionized the banking industry, the insurance industry, the distribution industry. The computer created the credit card industry and whole new industries based on databases and data processing.

Computer technology, as an aside, also provides another argument for small-company stocks. It used to be that big companies had the advantage because their expensive mainframe computer systems gave them faster information, which allowed them to control their operations more efficiently. But the microcomputer has meant that centralization no longer matters; what corporate America's fervor for downsizing and decentralization is saying is that very large companies no longer have an advantage.

Modern computer technology puts small companies in the big league.

Cheap computers and communications have made bank automatic teller machines possible. Most of us like to do business with an ATM rather than a bank teller, because the ATM is in a convenient location, is available twenty-four hours a day, is accurate and confidential, and doesn't make you stand in line. The ATM has also been a tremendous boon to banks. Banks that wanted to gain deposits and generate business around the city used to have to open a network of branches. Dozens of small offices were expensive to run. Today, most of that banking can be done with an ATM machine stuck in a gas station, a grocery store, or a street kiosk. Not having to lay out for bricks and mortar has allowed banks to close many of their neighborhood branches and still serve their customers, which has translated into higher earnings. In addition, when a bank is just a node in the computer network system that issues your ATM card and your credit card, bank mergers make logical sense; banks are acquired at generous prices. We have owned the shares of banks in Salt Lake City, Seattle, Memphis, and Honolulu.

The slot machine and the ATM are quite similar microcomputers under the skin. If you like, you can think of the ATM as a slot machine with a boring payoff. Alternatively, the slot machine can be considered the ultimate user-friendly computer. (Not so friendly, I admit, once your money runs out.) A growing percentage of casino gamblers prefer the machines to dealing with humans at table games (craps, blackjack, roulette), so casinos have been removing the tables to make more room for the slots. The one-armed bandit maker takes a very simple microcomputer, puts a display and coin box on it, and calls it a slot machine. If the company sold it as a computer, it would probably get $800 for it; selling it as a slot machine, it gets $6,000. Hence my continued affection for International Game Technology, the world leader in the manufacture of slot machines.

An ATM is a slot machine with a boring payoff.

The credit card, too, which has revolutionized consumer behavior in the last couple of decades, couldn't have existed without the changes in processing technology. A major reason consumer credit has expanded so rapidly is that you don't have to apply for a personal loan at the bank; just run up your card balance. We've owned three companies that issue credit cards: Advanta, First USA, and MBNA.

Producers of industrial products have had their lives changed by microprocessors, too, though their technology is less familiar to us. Modern electronic devices have changed the economics of the oil and gas industry, for example, by making it much cheaper for companies to find oil and gas. As accessible fields, like those in east Texas, are depleted, oil companies must either drill deeper wells or go to difficult locations like Alaska or the North Sea. You'd think the costs of finding oil would therefore rise. Instead, oil-finding costs have been going down. New technology—called 3-D seismic—allows oilmen to make images of underground structures by computerized methods very similar to the way radiologists make CAT scans of your lower back. The seismic charts can pinpoint likely oil or gas pools, so the driller can hit pay dirt with far fewer dry holes and find productive areas in fifty-year-old fields that were thought exhausted. Even offshore, space satellites can confirm the position of drill ships within a few yards. Oil and gas companies have also benefited from new technologies that allow horizontal drilling, reservoir modeling, subsea completions—all of which have lowered finding costs. As I mentioned in the last chapter, I've invested in some of the smaller companies that use the new technology to tap marginal properties sold off by the majors.

And then there are the companies that put together invaluable databases. Among the stocks we've owned are IMS International, which owns a proprietary computer database servicing the pharmaceutical industry, and Information Resources, a Chicago company that produces sophisticated market research data using point-of-sale scanners and high-speed data processing.

Recognizing a transforming technology and then investing downstream from it should be a key concept for any direct stock investor.

One future downstream possibility has me worried, however. Someday you'll be able to go into a computer store and pay $80 for a "Portfolio Manager" program, and I'll be out of business.

Future Pastures

What, then, might the next transforming technology be? The Internet would have to be at the top of the list. The product of the marriage of personal computing with fiber-optic data transmission, this baby is a real innovation—a low-cost, high-speed, worldwide, universally accessible communications system. It is already changing the world in many areas.

POLITICS

Tyrants always try to maintain a monopoly on information in order to control their population. State-controlled newspapers and broadcasting are an integral part of dictatorships. The governments prohibit messages from outside by jamming broadcasts and forbidding printed material from entering the country. That doesn't work in an Internet world. The student revolt in China was coordinated by data network. Tiananmen Square was cleared by troops, but the ideas of an open society remain.

What will be the next transforming technology? The Internet would have to head the list.

MANUFACTURING

When a minor bug was discovered in the Intel Pentium microprocessor chip, Intel tried to downplay the fault, but an enormous protest over the Internet forced a product recall.

PUBLISHING

The drawback with technical journals has always been the delay between the cry of "Eureka!" in the laboratory and the date of publication. It took time to write an article and have a journal accept, edit, and distribute it. In a fast-moving field, who wants to wait two years to receive the latest research? Today, researchers put their work on the Internet first. By the time the journal article or PhD thesis is finally published, all the people who need to know about it saw it the year before. The published journal is flipped into the library as archival material, not circulated for careful reading. Companies that publish trade journals realize that they have been marginalized, and so are trying to find a new role as editors of on-line papers.

MARKETING

Big companies control the information flow about a product through large marketing budgets, strong brands, and wide distribution. With the Internet, small companies can now compete against giants. Take the mutual fund industry as an example. Big-load funds used to dominate the business, because of the size of their advertising budgets and their ability to pay an army of brokers to sell their funds. Today, services such as Morningstar provide objective data on thousands of mutual funds through print, disk, and network delivery. Every fund gets one page, regardless of asset size, which equalizes giants and pygmies. The armored knights couldn't beat armies of commoners with muskets, and the corporate nobility of today is similarly vulnerable to upstart companies with smart, energetic, and competitive management.

One can see how the Internet will eventually transform the process of matching customer with product or service in field after field. It's going to affect the livings of a host of people one of these days. Who needs an insurance broker if you want a standard policy and are looking only for the lowest rate, and everybody's quotes are available on-line? Why consult a travel agent if you can call up vacation ideas, destination descriptions, and room rates on your PC screen? Why wait three weeks for a bookstore to get you a title it doesn't have in stock when a search of all sources can be immediate and the book shipped that day? If you are an insurance agent, travel agent, or bookstore owner, you had best rethink your livelihood, perhaps concentrating on improving the quality of the service you deliver.

The Internet has already brought many changes, but many more await. As I write these thoughts, in 1996, stocks directly associated with Internet, such as Netscape, America Online, UUNet, and Spyglass, have been bid to extravagant heights. It is time to look downstream, but it is not yet clear where the big money will be made.

8

THE PORTFOLIO JIGSAW, STOCK BY STOCK

There's an old riddle that serves as a nice logic test for children. Suppose you're on a long car trip, trying to prevent backseat warfare among three children, ages six, ten, and fourteen. This riddle offers the chance of preserving peace between Altoona and Pittsburgh.

Ask the three fidgeters the following question:

"Suppose we visit a coal mine. It's an underground mine, and two miners have come up the shaft in an elevator as we arrive. We see them get out of the elevator car and head for the locker room. One miner has a clean face, but the other miner has a dirty face. Which one will wash his face?"

The six-year-old doesn't hesitate: "Why, the one with the dirty face, silly. He has to wash it or his mommy will be mad at him when he gets home."

"Good," you reply. "Mommy taught you right. With such good manners, you can be a stockbroker when you grow up."

Then, about thirty seconds later, the ten-year-old shouts (ten-year-olds only shout), "No, I get it. The two men will look at each other. The man with the dirty face will see his friend is clean, so he'll figure his face is clean, too. But the miner with the clean face will look at the man with the dirty face and decide he must have a dirty face, too, so the clean man will be the one who washes."

"Excellent," you respond, smiling. "You know that most people mirror what someone else does, instead of doing what is best for them. You could be a good security analyst."

All is then quiet for about a half hour, when the fourteen-year-old suddenly bellows, "No way, Dad! Your riddle totally sucks. I mean, get a life, Dad. Like, if one of your miners got so dirty, how could the other nerd stay clean? What a screwed-up mine in your mind! You must think I'm a total loser or something."

"Well, well," you say. "If you knew how to tie a necktie and fiddle an expense account, you could be a great portfolio manager someday, especially if you learn to speak English. I think what you said was that my silly riddle was based on a faulty assumption, for certainly both miners would have had to be equally clean or dirty. I wish I could see through some of the riddles of real-world investing as easily as you demolished my riddle."

If you don't look at companies with a fresh perspective, you can't hope to find stocks that are priced below their true value. Coming up with broad trends and themes is a satisfying intellectual challenge, but then comes the nitty-gritty—finding the best companies to exploit those themes. That means both understanding the companies—their products, industry position, financials, and management—and deciding if their market price does or does not fairly reflect their value and prospects.

It is painstaking, often tedious, certainly not particularly glamorous work. If it's glamour you want, maybe you should take up gambling. A lot of people treat the stock market as though it's a casino. They buy a company because its stock's ticker symbol is the same as their wife's initials. Or the treasurer of the company is married to their cousin's brother-in-law. Something like that. Their reasons for owning a stock are very superficial, and when you do superficial things, you usually get nailed. The odds may be more on your side than at the casino—after all, stocks tend to go up more than down—but if you *really* treat the market as a casino, I'm not sure.

Unless you look at companies with a fresh perspective, you can't hope to find stocks that are priced below their true value.

As a matter of fact, gambling can throw some light on the nature of the investment process. Tens of millions of people get a big thrill out of gambling. They fill the casinos, excited by the wheels and whims of fortune. But there's no glamour in running a gambling casino. It's a boring and laborious job, no more exciting than running an iron foundry. The casino managers have to deal with expense controls, personnel, ad campaigns, all the usual demands. They have to give minute attention to details, the same as other business executives. But, laborious and boring as it may be, it happens to be where money is made. The people who are coming into the casinos to have excitement and thrills are transferring their money to people who are following laborious, boring routines.

That's my metaphor for security analysis. Most of it is just plain, hard detail work. It's like doing low-order police work, if you will—making phone calls, checking sources, trying to figure out what's going on.

Gamblers have lucky streaks, but over time the people who are patient and who take care with their investments will do better than those who just look upon the market as a horse race.

Idea Generation

Any mutual fund manager has no trouble coming up with portfolio candidates. The brokerage firms send us stacks of reports on companies, and their salesmen, who have a fairly good idea of the kinds of stocks we like, call about anything of special interest. We read trade journals as well as the usual business and financial publications. Executives at companies we call on often suggest we look into another company, usually a supplier or customer, but occasionally a competitor. And at analyst luncheons and other occasions we trade-talk with portfolio managers and analysts at other firms.

Though a professional gets more stock ideas thrown at him than does the individual investor, the average person who wants to invest directly in stocks (rather than take the mutual fund route) is exposed to more than enough of them. His broker, *The Wall Street Journal, Barron's, Forbes,* and other publications, friends who are investors, and contacts in his own line of business will keep him in supply.

And I believe Peter Lynch's I-get-my-ideas-at-the-mall approach works, too. Consumers can latch onto a lot of fine companies. Maybe a light went on for you the first time you waited in line for a cup of coffee at Starbucks. Or when the guys in the locker room started talking up Big Bertha drivers; Callaway Golf turned out to be another great stock. I well remember in my first years of training under Irving Harris when his first wife, Rosetta, came back from the supermarket with a couple of six-packs of Diet-Rite Cola, because she said all her friends were talking about it. It was the first diet cola. Irv, his antenna out, bought a position in Royal Crown Cola, the maker of Diet-Rite and a big winner.

No, coming up with names is not the problem. It's deciding which to discard and which to buy and how long to hold on to them that takes the work. You'll be lost if you don't bring some discipline to the process of evaluating companies and their stocks, for, as noted earlier, a great company isn't necessarily a great stock.

Even if you are a mutual fund shareholder rather than a direct buyer of stocks, you should be aware of investing methods to decide if your fund managers are conducting their business in a manner that makes sense to you. Prospectuses, recent fund reports, and press coverage can supply you with sufficient information about how different managers take care of money.

As for my own approach, I cannot overemphasize that I believe in entrepreneurially managed small companies that are benefiting from an important economic, social, or technological trend and whose domination of a niche promises superior earnings growth. And that I acquire them only if I can get them at a reasonable price.

To state my investment philosophy more succinctly, I want the companies I invest in to rest on a solid tripod. They must show evidence of

- Growth potential
- Financial strength
- Fundamental value

The first two obviously require analyzing the company; the last relates the company to its current market price.

Growth Potential

Growth potential implies many virtues, for a company can't be growing if it doesn't have fine products, an expanding market for those products, and the ability to efficiently manufacture and market them.

The best assurance of continued growth, and high profit margins, comes back to this: the company should have a special niche in the marketplace, so that sales don't depend on offering a commodity item at a lower price than the competition's. It should, to the degree possible, dominate that niche. The best company in a marginal industry is worth more than the third-best company in a major industry. I'd rather own shares of Hokuto, the leading mushroom grower in Japan, than of Mitsubishi Motors or Subaru.

The best company in a marginal industry is worth more than the third-best company in a major industry.

The types of niches, too, haven't changed in the twenty-five years I've been in the batter's box: they can be technological, based on marketing prowess, or reflect a geographical monopoly or near monopoly, like that of a TV station, newspaper, or regional shopping mall. Nobody can import the *Home Town Gazette* from Taiwan.

Glamour has nothing to do with a niche's appeal. A dull business run by a good businessman is far better than a glamorous business with mediocre management. And even if the glamorous business is run by a genius, often, in that kind of industry, its competitors are also geniuses, so nobody has an advantage, as I've commented about high-tech companies.

A dull business run by a good businessman is far better than a glamorous business with mediocre management.

Usually the market pays what you might call an entertainment tax, a premium, for stocks with an exciting story. So boring stocks sell at a discount. Buy enough of them and you can cover your losses in high tech.

In Chapter 3, as an example of a once ugly duckling finally recognized as a swan, I discussed Newell Industries, in the business of making sexy items like frying pans and drapery hooks. It's been one of my biggest successes. Under the theme of *outsourcing* we looked at Worthington Industries, a fine company, but steel warehousing doesn't exactly set the pulse racing. My colleague Chuck McQuaid has always liked Douglas & Lomason. It makes automobile seats, which is about as low-tech as you can get. The company was acquired in 1996, bringing us a handsome profit.

"Boring" stocks sell at a discount. Buy enough of them and you can cover your losses in high tech.

Terry Hogan, another teammate, loves Baldor Electric, a maker of electric motors, a seemingly uninspiring commodity business. But by developing a line of specialty motors, Baldor has managed to create a strong niche position in a highly competitive industry. Another of Terry's favorites is Unifi. Texturizing fibers is hardly showbiz either, but Unifi does it better than anyone else.

Who's in Charge?

My favorite test for a stock I'm interested in I call my "quit test."

I pretend that someone has called me and told me that First National Bank has just authorized a line of credit sufficient for me to buy all the stock in this company at current market value. Am I willing to leave my mutual funds and take over and run the company?

Most of the time my answer is, "Hell, no." But every once in a while I say to myself, "God, I bet I really could do something with this company." Those are the stocks I buy with the greatest conviction and excitement.

I used to work with a brokerage analyst who covered a company called Systems & Computer Technology. Acorn owned the stock, so we talked to this nice young man frequently. One day he told me, "I'm not going to be talking to you again as an analyst." I asked him, "What happened? Did you get indicted again?" He laughed and told me, "No, I'm going to work for Systems & Computer Technology." What an endorsement! I bought more of the stock.

Very often, a small company is exciting because its management is exciting, which is why I sometimes fantasize about the challenge of running a company myself. Superior managers can really exploit a niche and sustain high profitability. Is there a professional investor anywhere—at least any who invests on company fundamentals instead of stock momentum or chart revelations—who doesn't profess that he puts great store in "good management"? But it's hardly ever defined. Too often among Wall Street research departments it means glib management. Analysts praise the managers who cooperate with them, who reveal titillating goodies, such as monthly sales figures. Taciturn management is definitely *not* considered good.

Good management to Wall Street also means nothing more than a company with three consecutive quarters of rising earnings. Make it four quarters and you have *great* management.

But exciting performance numbers by themselves aren't enough to qualify managers as superior, at least not in my book. One good year or two could be a fluke. Or maybe current management's predecessors set operations up so well that the incumbents haven't had time to wreck everything. If you judge management solely by a company's numbers and then pay more for the stock because of "good management," you are guilty of what bridge players call the double-counting of face cards.

I also know that good management is not a science. I have a master's degree in industrial management from MIT, that monument of science, and I can tell you that management definitely does not qualify as one of the scientific disciplines. What it relies on, when good, is a knowledge of psychology (not an exact science either), common sense, and an equable disposition. The good manager is able to get other people to work in the same general direction that he or she is and makes sure that direction is a sensible one. Changing the direction of a company takes *really* good management.

If you judge management solely by a company's numbers and then pay more for the stock because of "good management," you are guilty of what bridge players call the double-counting of face cards.

Judging management's competence is a challenge, because it's not easy to find out what goes on inside a company. It's like marriages. We're all surprised to learn that the friends we thought were the perfect couple have just filed for divorce. I don't know how many times I've mentioned to someone that his or her company has a reputation for fine management, only to hear a laugh and "You should only know."

It's particularly hard for the individual investor to find out much about management. Annual reports can be useful, give you a sense of the integrity and vision of the chairman and his policy makers, but you have to remember that what is most important may be precisely what the company *doesn't* want you to read. If you know someone who works in the company, or sells to it, or competes with it, you may be able to get better information. It helps considerably if you have followed a company for a while. If in its 1992 annual report the company ballyhooed its six new stores in California as "the launching of a new division for which we have the highest expectations," and the 1996 report boasts as evidence of "strong financial controls" its decision to close its California stores, you might suspect that management is applying spin control to a failure.

It takes digging to get the full story, and most individual investors don't have the time for it and wouldn't be particularly interested even if they did have the time. That's why we have mutual funds. The professional's biggest advantage is access to top management. We can ask tough questions and make judgments about how the people answer them. We seldom buy a stock at Acorn unless I or someone on my staff visits the company.

One would think that with all those brokerage firms out there dispatching their analysts to every corner of corporate America, we portfolio managers could just sit at our desks and sift through research reports while drinking latte. Analysts are competent gatherers of facts and figures, but few can be relied upon for much more. Their assessments of managements are superficial and far too uncritical. Many even submit their write-ups to companies for editing. You'd think they'd been hired to do public relations. A sell recommendation? Most of the ratings they offer are *Buy Now, Buy Pretty Soon,* and *Buy on Dips.* It's like reading *Pravda* in Stalin's day: any adjective less upbeat than "superior" is code for "disaster."

I know some investors say they prefer not talking to management, because managers are always too optimistic and they don't want to be swayed by overly rosy forecasts. But I've found these visits very valuable. You do get a better sense of the company and the honesty and ability of the people running it. Management is a particularly critical factor at smaller companies. I like to think that, as an investor, I'm going to be the partners of these entrepreneurs for a long time, and I sure as heck want to meet my partners.

So I like to find managements that I feel are my surrogates. I want a small group of hard workers who know their industry, who have plans for the future but can adapt to change, and who are shareholder oriented, in large part because they own a large chunk of stock themselves. We always ask around, get third-party opinions from the company's suppliers and customers and others in the same industry, but I've found that in most instances I can get a tolerable sense of the ability of managers after spending some time with them. It's not much different from the way you decide if your plumber is honest and competent.

As for their too-optimistic predictions, I can usually discern whether top brass estimates high—or low, for that matter, for some managers will say the company should earn $1.60 when it will probably do $2. You can also build some kind of rapport in face-to-face meetings that makes it easier to keep checking on the company, and to get the lowdown on competitors, customers, and suppliers, which can lead to other stock ideas.

Yes, it's tough to spend time out of the office calling on companies, though the senior people of many come through Chicago to address a group of analysts or even drop into our offices. If an analyst sees two companies a week—which is an easy load—he sees one hundred a year, and with several analysts on staff, you can keep up with a considerable universe. When abroad, you can often manage to see four or five companies in one day.

Managements can be guarded about what they tell you, but their competitors will usually talk freely about them.

Visiting a company doesn't mean you have to—or even want to—*own* that company. Some of the most valuable information we pick up about an industry comes from talking to companies we'll probably never own. They may be competitors of companies we do own. Managements can be guarded, especially if they know we own a lot of their stock. But their competitors will usually talk freely about them.

It's like trying to find out about a young lady you are interested in. If you ask her mother, you are certainly going to get a different perspective than you would if you asked the boyfriend she just broke up with. We like to hear what the old boyfriend has to say.

Sometimes management impresses me so strongly that I'll make a bet on the people even if the numbers don't meet my usual requirements. A couple of years ago I bought the stock of a new company called Catalyst Energy, put together by former Salomon Brothers investment bankers to develop hydroelectric plants and cogeneration facilities. The company was finally earning a few pennies, but with the stock at 11, the P/E was astronomical. It was also nearly impossible to predict what the company might earn in the future. For me it was a poetic stock, a bet on management. I had a feeling they were onto something, and at first the enterprise and the stock did well. But then the company went downhill and, eventually, into bankruptcy. What happened? The executives began to feel rich and, while indulging in the perks of wealth, neglected the business before it was sufficiently established.

Financial Strength

Financial strength—low debt, adequate working capital, conservative accounting—makes corporate growth sustainable.

First, look at a company's balance sheet to see if there's too much debt, or rising debt. There's nothing wrong with debt per se; it's one way you can expand a company rapidly. What constitutes too much of it is a function of the kind of company you're looking at. A consumer loan company, for example, has to carry a debt load that would be totally inappropriate for a cyclical manufacturing company. If you're the latter with a heavy load of debt, you'll go broke when demand slackens, and that's a very bad idea for shareholders. You read in the papers about such failures during every recession. Generally, if the debt of any kind of manufacturing or retail business is more than half of the company's total capitalization, there's a problem.

You also have to worry about what else is on the balance sheet. Look at the size of pension liabilities, for example. I want to see if the company is generating cash or simply accounting earnings. A lot of companies have some sort of goodwill or intangibles on their balance sheet that I may want to write down in my analysis. Examine inventories and receivables and their relation to revenues, and keep an especially sharp eye out for changes in those numbers. If a company normally has inventories running 25 percent of sales and suddenly you see inventories at 50 percent of sales, you'd better start asking some questions. It's possible the company is expanding rapidly and sales haven't shown up at its stores yet; that could be all right, just a sign of growth. But many times it's a sign of impending doom. It means the company has a growing stockpile of merchandise it can't sell.

If a company's inventories normally run 25 percent of sales and suddenly inventories rise to 50 percent of sales, you'd better start asking some questions.

Financial strength is usually a virtue of companies that have been around awhile and are doing reasonably well, which is why I rarely invest in turnarounds, start-ups, or initial public offerings. What some people pay for glamorous IPOs never ceases to amaze me. I remember when biotechnology companies, such as Genentech and Cetus, first became public companies, back in the late seventies and early eighties. I understood that such marvelous-sounding technologies as recombinant DNA and monoclonal antibodies have enormous potential for future growth, so I took a very good look at the stocks.

Genentech, back in early 1980, was selling at about $43, with no earnings. If in ten years, I figured, Genentech should have $38 million in annual profits ($5 per share) and sell at twenty-four times earnings (the price-earnings ratio at that time of well-regarded Schlumberger), the stock would rise to $120. This highly speculative outcome would represent an annual rate of gain over the ten years of only 10.8 percent. At that time you could buy a ten-year government bond with a yield of 12.4 percent, so Genentech failed to meet the value test. It was a simple test, and the stock failed it, but common sense is left behind when people are bedazzled by a concept. And there was no hotter concept at the time than biotech.

You can look at high-flying stocks this way all the time, and you should. In 1996 Terry Hogan became interested in a company called ThermoLase, which was opening salons that remove body hair by laser. The business concept was solid, with real growth potential. But a little time spent analyzing the numbers brought us back to reality. ThermoLase had opened only a few stores, had revenues of less than $30 million, and was barely breaking even. But its premise so excited investors they had bid its stock up to a price, $24, where it was already a billion-dollar company. Even if ThermoLase's expansion plans are fulfilled, we couldn't see the stock's selling ten years from now at a figure that would give investors more than a very modest annual return. Stick with proven companies, like Carnival Corporation, an industry leader with a $9 billion capitalization but $2 billion in revenues, $1.80 a share in earnings, and a long record of 20 percent yearly earnings growth.

Fundamental Value

Fundamental value means that stocks are a buy only if they are cheap, but you can measure cheapness in two ways. You can look at a stock's price in relation to a company's replacement cost, what it would take to reproduce its assets. Or you can concentrate on the company's earnings-growth prospects. A company's earnings may be flat but its stock cheap in terms of its underlying worth; or its market capitalization may be higher than the value of its assets, but its earnings potential still labels it a bargain.

Growth stock investors, of course, concentrate on earnings, and a stock's price-to-earnings ratio is their most commonly used yardstick in measuring a stock's attractiveness. But you can also compare price to sales, or to cash flow. With a company that's highly profitable, and whose profitability is recognized by the market, it doesn't matter: the multiples will be high no matter which ratio you look at.

P/Es can be tricky, though. Sometimes they mean little. In a turnaround situation, most obviously, a company could be losing money but be attractive because of the promise of future profits. The earnings part of the P/E equation can be manipulated by compliant accountants. You have to be particularly cautious in evaluating real estate companies: reported earnings can be totally misleading because of illusory depreciation numbers.

In some industries—oil, for example—you may see accounting losses but strong cash flow. Cash flow—or, as analysts now refer to it, EBITDA (earnings before interest, taxes, depreciation, and amortization)—is a good way to get a handle on the operating profitability of a company, and probably the best tool for comparing companies, especially those in different industries or countries. The German brewery Binding Brauerei, whose stock my wife and associate, Leah Zell, bought when it was selling at about thirty times earnings (according to German accountants), was priced at only three times cash flow.

Chuck McQuaid recently pointed out that "perhaps the most common mispricing occurs when other analysts aggregate all of a company's disparate operations together and apply a valuation multiple to the total earnings or cash flow." One division incurring start-up costs could be dragging down total earnings, distorting what is fundamentally a healthy picture. As Chuck notes, a "private market value model allows us to disaggregate business segments and uncover 'hidden value.'" We call this the *good company/bad company* theme. The good part of the company is worth more than the stock is selling for. Fix or sell the bad part and the stock can take off.

We pay considerable attention to a company's asset value. That's different from book value. Book value is the cost of the company's assets minus depreciation. It's a funny number. In today's world it's often a residual of taking an old number—from such a long time ago that it doesn't mean much—and making rather arbitrary additions and subtractions to it as time goes by. It's an easy number to find, but often a treacherous measure.

Consider the Rouse Company, a real estate company. Its properties have depreciated to the point that the company's book value is negligible, yet the actual economic value of Rouse's shopping centers is quite high. One could find that Rouse has a book value of only $2 or $3 a share, but that its asset value—the real market value—is $25 or $30 a share. Asset value takes everything into consideration, including the company's long- and short-term liabilities and intangible assets such as brands and patents. It better reflects the company's true private market value, what a potential acquirer would be willing to pay for the company. Try to invest in companies that you'd be happy to buy lock, stock, and barrel at their current price.

Try to invest in companies that you'd be happy to buy lock, stock, and barrel at their current price.

But one of the legs of my investment tripod is *growth potential.* As I often say, I want it all. I look for companies that are still cheap in relation to their earnings-growth potential. When you invest in smaller companies, you can still find them.

Funes the Memorious

One would think that Ireneo Funes—who could look at or hear something once and instantly recall every detail at any time in the future—would be the ideal security analyst. "His perception and his memory were infallible. We, at one glance, can perceive three glasses on a table; Funes, all the leaves and tendrils and fruit that make up a grapevine." One glance at a financial statement would have been sufficient for him to memorize it forever and to recall instantly any item on the report.

Mr. Funes is not available for hiring, since he lived near Montevideo, died in 1889, and was the fictional invention of Jorge Luis Borges, the late, distinguished Argentine writer. However, even if Ireneo had freed himself from those three technical difficulties and applied in person to the Acorn Fund, his perfect memory would still not make him a good analyst. Borges admitted that Funes "was not very capable of thought. To think is to forget differences, generalize, make abstractions. In the teeming world of Funes, there were only details, almost immediate in their presence."

Funes, paralyzed by his overwhelming knowledge of detail, contributed no useful insights. Real people, with imperfect perceptions, can produce ideas, usually in the form of metaphors. As Jacob Bronowski pointed out in *The Origins of Knowledge and Imagination*, Newton found the law of gravity when he saw the moon as a ball thrown around the earth.

When it comes to investments, we can never learn every detail about a company, as Funes the Memorious could. Still, we can try to understand the sources of profit and growth in a company, the plans and philosophy of the management, the competitive environment, and the negatives that might alter its prospects. I always try to express my reason for owning a stock in a short, clear statement, such as "Expansion of the hotel and casino business will double the company's earnings in two years." And it controls our sell decisions as well. When the statement is no longer valid, the stock should be sold.

Applying the Scales

To help us determine whether or not a stock is cheap in light of its earnings prospects—or, put another way, what the company's potential is worth in current dollars—my firm, like many institutional managers, uses a dividend discount model. We first input what our analysts think the company's earnings-growth rate will be (since dividends are paid out of earnings). This is an estimate, it is true. About as far as we'll try to predict specific earnings is two years into the future, and even that time frame is difficult. There is a tendency to overestimate probable earnings, because the stocks you buy are the ones you are most optimistic about. The people actively buying a stock are the ones who believe the company is doing great things. Prices are set by optimists. You have to remind yourself of that fact and leave room for disappointments.

Then we have to put into the model a figure representing interest rates—the return we will forgo by owning the stock instead of a bond. If you come up with an earnings-per-share figure for two years hence, then you have to decide what multiple the market will put on those earnings to arrive at a likely market price, and when interest rates are high, multiples are lower.

We tend to overestimate the probable earnings of our stocks, because we buy the ones we like best. Prices are set by optimists.

One way to define an interest rate is to see it as a message from the future to the present; the rate tells us how much a promise of money in the future is worth now. We know that if inflation is high—and interest rates will therefore be high as well—current dollars will be worth less in the future. A reverse process determines present values. If interest rates go to very high levels, present values go down. Discounted at 12 percent a year—the interest rate in 1980, for example—a promise of $100 in twenty years is worth only $10 now. That's why in the mid-eighties, when interest rates dropped back from 12 percent to 7 percent and the worth of $100 promised in twenty years climbed to $26, P/Es and stock prices shot up. Growth stocks, most of whose payoff is in the future, went up faster than dividend-paying value stocks.

So our model gives us a likely price for the stock two years hence, given our earnings estimates and a P/E that reflects an interest rate assumption; then we can compare that target price, and a probable rate of return for the two years, to what most analysts are expecting. A stock is cheap, and a probable buy, if our expectations are higher than the consensus.

We can prove wrong in our assumptions, of course. It's a land mine problem: If you have soldiers advancing against the enemy, chances are high that most of your soldiers will make it across the minefield and win the battle. But you know you are going to lose some men; you just don't know which ones. In our investment battles, we know some investment ideas will get blown up and overall performance won't be as good as we'd hoped.

A chart is a handy, shorthand way of checking up on a stock. If you see it's doubled in the past six months, you're probably too late.

Do I also look at charts to help me in making buy decisions? I do. I'd never buy a stock solely on the basis of its "breaking out" or anything of that sort, but a chart is a handy, shorthand way of checking up on what's been going on in the stock. If you see a stock has doubled in the past six months, you're probably too late.

Can Machine-Made Be Better?

Like almost everyone else these days, we rely on computers throughout the investment process—to organize data, screen for certain characteristics, and make calculations, including those of our dividend discount model. We're using them only as research assistants, though, and not in a particularly sophisticated or creative way. They're good at screening and evaluating for us, looking through data the same way human beings do. We're not using them to predict where the market's headed or to pick stocks or to construct a portfolio.

Someday the technical people—the "quants"—relying entirely

on databases and their computers, may outperform those of us who rely on fundamental analysis, who call on managements and make subjective judgments. Most quants, however, will at best achieve only reasonable results. If the market produces 10 percent a year, the computer-based program may produce 10.5 percent.

Some quants claim they are doing that now, but whether their methods will work over time isn't clear, because reversion to the mean often takes a while. These systems are hard to test. Even if you've been right time after time, there's still a probability, however small, of a wipeout that's in the system somewhere. It isn't hard to set up a process with a high probability of a small win and a low probability of an enormous loss. Some gamblers play only red at the roulette wheel, doubling their bet every time they lose; but eventually black comes up ten times in a row, wiping them out.

Computers can find a trend that's been in place for a couple of years and that may persist for another few but then suddenly disappear, because it wasn't really there in the first place.

Another question is whether the computer-driven system is generating the results, supplying a real edge, or is just what academics call a "data-mining situation." You can make your computer run a multiple regression program on a thousand different time series. If you look at enough of these runs, you are bound to find one that seems to predict the stock market. Data mining, in short, will come up with exciting patterns, but they are merely coincidental. Computers find a trend that's been in place for a couple of years and may persist for another few but then suddenly disappear, because it wasn't really there in the first place.

After all, if a system is eventually discovered that beats the market, then more and more people will use it, and whatever advantage there was will be absorbed into the market and disappear.

A good example is the so-called January Effect. As noted earlier, over time small-company stocks have outperformed blue chip stocks. A large portion of this superior behavior has taken place in January—or, more precisely, the last two days in December and the first week of January. This odd occurrence was quite reliable—and useful—until it was discovered and broadcast. After two professors published a breathless book about the January Effect,* it fled the scene and ceased to be a reliable event.

So far I've done well with my old-fashioned ways, though it's become a good deal tougher to get an edge and make unusual money in the U.S. market, with information transmitted so rapidly that everybody knows everything at the same time. I am reminded of John Henry, who, you may remember from the song, was "a steel-driving man" capable of pounding in railroad spikes at an astonishing rate. One day they matched him against a newfangled steam drill, and sure enough, he beat the machine. But only one day in a row. On the second day the steam drill was just as able to drive spikes as it had been on the first day, but John Henry had exhausted himself. "He laid down his hammer and he died, Lord, Lord."

Is somebody going to come up with a computer version of a stock market steam drill that will beat everybody else—at least until others catch on and invent equally effective drills? I think the answer to that is maybe. I haven't seen it, but at some point it may happen. I guess at that juncture I will just lay down my hammer and meet my Lord.

---

*Robert A. Haugen and Josef Lakonishok, *The Incredible January Effect: The Stock Market's Unsolved Mystery* (Homewood, Ill.: Dow-Jones-Irwin, 1988).

Stock Mate

In February 1996 Gary Kasparov, the reigning world chess champion, faced one of his toughest opponents: Deep Blue, an IBM computer said to be able to sort through 100 million positions a second. The champ won, but it wasn't a KO: the computer took the first game in the six-game match and managed two draws.

In another ten years the machine will probably triumph. Computer chess is getting better over time much faster than people chess is getting better over time. Still, chess is so complex that there is no hope of any human or computer playing "perfect" chess. Humans have done fairly well at it, though. At least, few other creatures can beat them. If you play chess with your dog, you'll beat your dog. The dog's tail will probably knock the pieces off the board at some point, ending the game, but before then it is likely the dog will make some very bad moves.

In simpler games, such as checkers or backgammon, one could design a computer program that would always make a demonstrably "best" move, but this isn't possible in chess because of the enormous number of possible positions reachable in eight or ten future moves. Therefore, a chess program must use a set of heuristic principles to judge a position (control the center, protect the king), and the best chess program is the one with the most useful set of heuristics.

Chess was a good test for a computer, because chess is a game with a fixed number of rules. The rules stay unchanged, and there are no random elements. Because the rules are finite, they can be written into a computer, and the computer can evaluate positions. Computers have gotten better and better at it. In the early 1960s I played chess on a very large computer at Northwestern University, and I usually beat the machine. It wasn't on its optimal setting, but neither was I. Today, there are a number of $39.95 chess programs that are much better than I am.

The stock market is different from chess. The number of rules of the game is not known, and some of the rules change over time. There are seemingly random elements in the game, such as a war in the Mideast or a drought in the Midwest, which are impossible to predict. It would be a lot more difficult to write a chess program if sometimes the chessboard had sixty-four squares and the next thing you knew it had eighty-one. If the number of squares changed randomly over time, it would add to the complexity. If a system is open enough, you may have something that is not formally solvable on a computer.

There is no clear upside limit for computer investing, but the message of the chess metaphor is valid: investors proceed by heuristic rules (buy small company stocks, buy low-price-to-earnings-ratio stocks, buy companies with growing earnings), and the best investors will be those whose heuristics match the real world.

When to Let Go

In almost every press interview, I'm asked, "What are your sell criteria?" I say I have two: the too-early system and the too-late system. And both work with about equal inexactitude.

As earlier chapters made clear, I want to find stocks I can hold four or five years, in part because transaction costs are high when you buy and sell small-cap stocks and in part because I think I am better at identifying trends and stocks with staying power than I am at guessing a company's earnings for the next quarter or a stock's short-term behavior. So I am a reluctant seller.

Karl Popper, an Austrian who taught the philosophy of science at the London School of Economics, wrote that his idea of a good scientific theory is one that you could disprove in principle. If scientific theory says that pouring a glass of cold water on your head will make your face wet and cold, that is a "falsifiable" theory. You can take a glass of water and pour it on your head and see what happens. If in fact the water makes your face dry and warm, you have falsified your original theory. So the key in validating a scientific theory is to come up with a crucial experiment to test whether or not the theory holds up in practice.

Have a reason for buying every stock you own. As soon as that reason comes into doubt, ask yourself if it isn't time for a change.

When investing in stocks, you presumably have a reason for owning each one, and if the reason becomes falsifiable, then you must decide whether you should keep it for other justifications, or whether it's time for a change. As I mentioned in the story about Funes the Memorious, when we buy a stock we state the reason we bought it. In our database it might say, "I own Teva because it has a new drug for multiple sclerosis that's going to make the company grow very rapidly."

Now one of two things can happen. Maybe some hamsters in the lab get diarrhea and the drug goes into the ash can. Or the drug succeeds, the company makes a lot of money, and the stock goes from 10 to 50. In either case, the original reason for owning the stock has been falsified, and you sell (unless you can convince yourself that the company has another great product in the lab that will fuel further growth, or that Eli Lilly is dying to acquire the company).

One of the interesting things about that kind of analysis is that it tends not to rest on numbers alone. It certainly doesn't involve trying to guess what the market's going to do; you're talking only about the company. Even when the numbers somewhat disappoint, you can still ask yourself, "Overall, are the managers you bet on coming through pretty much as you'd hoped?" A portfolio manager who thinks this way will look for companies he really likes, businesses he wants to participate in, go into partnership with.

In real-life portfolio management, sell decisions are often tough. You can't really apply hard-and-fast rules. Instead, you have to continually reevaluate each situation. If a company's earnings come through lower than we expected, we go over our numbers, talk to management, and decide whether we were right; and we either stick with the company for the long pull—even buy more stock as its price drops on the disappointing news—or sell because we see now that our original premise was mistaken.

It is equally hard to decide what to do when the stock price has gone up. We started buying grand-slammer International Game Technology when it was selling at eight and ten times earnings. It rose to where it was selling at over forty times earnings, and I did some selling. When a stock is selling at forty times earnings, the company needs to be extraordinarily successful for the investor to earn an ordinary return. Our model will show that the stock has no return left in it, and the sell signal is clear.

Some may say that earnings growing at 25 percent a year justify a 40 P/E, but it's extremely difficult for a company to maintain that kind of growth, even for a short period of time, and no company can do it over a long period of time. If the company makes its 25 percent and the P/E stays the same, you could make 25 percent a year. But that's the absolute upside, because it would be rare indeed for the P/E to climb from 40 to 60. The downside looks scary, however. The simplest way to get hurt is illustrated, again, by what happened to IGT. The company's business remained great; earnings beat analysts' expectations. But the stock came down to fifteen times earnings because the overall market was weak and the gambling-stock craze waned; investors moved on to the next hot sector. A company's business can remain strong but you can still lose money.

Even worse, earnings can stumble—and on balance, they will. Studies have shown that if you take the ten companies with the highest expected growth rates over the next one to five years, you will have more failures to reach predicted levels than you will companies that exceed the analysts' targets. Analysts, too, get carried away. It's far too easy to take a piece of paper and write down 25 percent as a projected growth rate.

Earnings can stumble—and on balance, they will.

Those are the realities, and why we apply a value template to even the fastest growers.

What Shall We Do Today?

The money management business, my business, has a primary problem. Simply stated, it's "What am I going to do today?" The answer to that question sums up our investment process.

Most businesses don't have that problem. If you're running a coffee shop, you know very well what you have to do today. You have to come in and make sure you have six people on duty and that they are clean and well dressed. You have to see to it that the store is clean. You have to check inventory to be sure you have enough coffee and milk and cups and napkins. Then you open the door and the people line up and you make coffee for them. You basically follow a routine, and what has to be done tomorrow is very much like what has to be done today.

Now think about the office of a mutual fund manager or any other money manager. With a couple of hundred stocks in the portfolio and ten thousand other stocks out there that could be new or better investments, the key question is how you can get the most value out of your staff of expensive analysts. Where do you concentrate your efforts? How can you add some value? It's easy to do busywork or call companies you own and like and have easy access to, but that's not going to move you forward very much. Stocks are fairly priced most of the time, so if the analysts are going to do something useful, they'll have to spend their time looking for the ones that aren't, where their effort will make a difference. Those who come from a computer software background would regard it as a database problem.

At Acorn, we try to estimate rates of return for all the companies that have attracted us for one reason or another and that we know something about—six or seven hundred of them, including the ones we own; and the universe expands and contracts as we bring companies in and out of our focus. We review this list every week. It's clear that about a half-dozen possibilities for new investments really look as though they promise a high rate of return. Another bunch seems marginal.

We try to estimate the price range in which a stock ought to sell. As long as the stock is bouncing around within that range, that's fine. You want to sound the alarm bell only when stocks move outside that range, when all of a sudden your estimates and the market's estimates are severely different. However, the fact that a signal is flashing doesn't necessarily tell you what to do. It just tells you that something is going on, that it pays to put in some effort to try to figure out what's happening and likely to happen.

If you're manufacturing chocolate chip cookies, you don't look at every cookie. Instead, you install a machine that puts the chips in the cookies—say, seven to each—and down the line you set up an inspection station where you sample the cookies once in a while. If the cookies are coming through with seven bits, the green light stays on, but if all of a sudden a cookie comes through with five bits or nine, a red light goes on. You stop the machine and readjust the chocolate chip dispenser.

That is sort of what we do. We look at the stocks on our list, or already in our portfolio, only when the red light goes on, when other analysts' forecasts or actual earnings come through markedly different from our own forecasts. It tells us we have a funny cookie. It doesn't tell us whether there are too many chips or too few, but it tells us to pay attention, because something's going on. In the cookie bakery you call this method statistical quality control, a routine system in factories. We call it an outlier finding system, and our analysts focus on these anomalies.

We have expectations for each stock for the next couple of years, based on our analysts' earnings estimate and a likely future P/E for the stock. If the rest of the world thinks the company is going to make $1 a share—consensus estimates are readily available—and our analyst thinks it is going to make $1.30 a share, we've identified an outlier, and it's time to go back and figure out what's what. Most of the time, the rest of the world is probably right; $1 a share is a better estimate. Our analyst just hadn't gotten the word yet or hadn't fed the latest numbers into our model. Well, you change your own estimate and that fixes the problem.

But once in a while the analyst will say, "No, dammit, this company is going to do very well—better than people think. A buck thirty is closer to the mark." Then you have something that ought to be bought, if you don't already own it. And if the opposite happens with a stock you do own, it ought to be sold.

That's the way we decide how to spend our days. We concentrate on the controversial cases that can make a big difference.

Aureodigititis

All this constant checking and rechecking, this poring over financial statements and running around the country (and, these days, the world) talking to company executives is demanding work. If you aren't working hard at this terribly competitive business, you aren't going to do very well. But at times you can fool yourself. One of the main occupational diseases of professional investors—and it can strike anyone—I call "aureodigititis," the disease of the golden finger.

The way you are stricken is by looking at *The Wall Street Journal,* pointing your finger at Beefsteak Mines, and thinking, "I like that stock." You buy some and it goes up 30 percent. A month later, reading *Barron's,* you see a write-up of Amalgamated Conglomerate, and you say to yourself, "Sounds great. I love that company." You buy some and it goes up 40 percent. After this has happened a couple of times, you tell yourself, "This is a marvelous finger. Whatever I point this finger at turns into gold. What's more, with this magic finger I've got, I don't have to do my research so thoroughly. I've become a great intuitive stock picker." Aureodigititis has clearly reached an advanced state and, unless quickly diagnosed and treated, will bring disaster.

All this isn't as silly as it sounds, because the disease can strike anyone during a bull market. You begin to believe in your infallible genius. It's a terrible trap. Intuition, strengthened by experience, plays its role in the investment process, but there is no substitute for careful analysis. It's why most investors are better off in mutual funds that pay analysts to spend their days putting companies under the microscope.

9

░░░░░░░░░░░░░░░░░░░░░░░░░░░░░

IS THERE A TIME FOR TIMING?

I'll tell you a secret about my fellow professionals that I probably should not reveal: market timing is the secret vice of a lot of portfolio managers.

Whenever they are interviewed by the press, they put on their most solemn faces and proclaim: "Trying to predict what the market will do is a fool's game. We pay little attention to the market. All our attention is on the companies we own."

But constantly watching those companies (and talking to their managements about how business is going), tracking the economy, the market, the Fed, the dollar, consumer polls, and the reams of commentary we get from Wall Street strategists, not to mention engaging in shop talk with friends in the industry, we'd be brain-dead if we didn't develop some kind of opinion about where things are headed. And it colors, to varying degrees, how most of us run our portfolios. We hold back on new investments, we lighten up a bit, or, if our reading is positive, we get more aggressive.

I'm no better, I confess it. When asked by a reporter whether I think the next big move in the market will be up or down, I come back with some I-couldn't-care-less response like "Yeah, one of those." But back at my desk making buy-and-sell decisions, my bias will come out.

I will also tell you this: if I'd done no such tinkering, I'd have been better off.

I don't always have a notion of where the market's headed, but usually I do. I've found that sometimes I'm right and sometimes I'm wrong. All in all, my calls are useless. If I were always wrong, that would be terrific. Somebody could make a fortune using my forecasts as a reliable contrary indicator.

My market-timing predictions are useless.

Several years ago, in early January, our team in the office decided, over a cheerful lunch, to guess where the Dow Jones Industrial index, then at 2190, would be at the end of the year. We all jotted down our predictions and handed them in. I came up with 2316, and by a strange coincidence, my wife also picked 2316.

"How did you get *your* number?" I asked her.

"Well," she said, "my birthday is on the twenty-third and our daughter's is on the sixteenth, so . . ."

"Ridiculous!" I declared. "Mindless superstition!"

"Okay," said Leah, "so how did *you* pick 2316, Mr. Economic Forecaster?"

"Simple," I said. "My account number at the club is 2316."

As it happened, the Dow closed the year at 2342, so we hadn't done badly. Our methodologies were probably as reliable as most of the highly sophisticated predictive systems.

All of us would like to be able to sell all our stocks the day before a market crash. But how do you do it? Bombarded with, and confused by, divergent views in the media, many probably end up depending on their gut feel for where the market's headed. That's dangerous. They are too likely to absorb the prevailing mood, which leads to buying when the market's overheated and selling when pessimism reigns and prices are cheap.

Looking for more objective grounds than instinct, timers turn to charts and "indicators"—a packet of economic, business, and market statistics. Some individual investors keep track of such things on their own, but most haven't the time or patience and rely instead on market gurus—their broker's in-house strategist, a newsletter writer, or someone quoted in the morning paper. The first clue that should make you suspect that it's not going to be all that easy to foretell the market's future is that all the prognosticators start with the same material but end up with wildly different scenarios. What data you select and how you weight and massage them can radically change the output. But even at those rare times when most of the seers agree on where the market's headed, it has a perverse habit of galloping off in the opposite direction.

The Past as False Messenger

The reason for this habit is simply that the charts and indicators are all designed to predict what's coming based on what's happened in the past, and past experience is shaky ground upon which to build expectations. Everybody who does market timing has a set of signals he follows because they worked the last time. The trouble comes when they just don't work the next time.

In *The Art of Conjecture,* political philosopher Bertrand de Jouvenel noted that we tend

> to postulate that tomorrow will be the same as today; likewise, when we are aware of movement, we assume that tomorrow will differ from today *in the same way* as today differs from yesterday. . . . [Such assumptions] exert a strong sway

over our minds. The lifespan of man has become longer; it will become still longer. The number of work hours in the year has decreased; it will decrease yet further. The standard of living has risen; it will rise even more. Whatever the precise reasons given to justify each such assumption, they are brought in only to justify this immediate and spontaneous conviction—things will be *that* way, for they have already gone *that* way. The sharper our awareness of a past movement, the stronger our conviction of its future continuation.

De Jouvenel might have added that we also give greater credence to events of the past when they seem to confirm our desires for the future. Thucydides understood that syndrome: "The usual thing among men is that when they want something, they will, without any reflection, leave that to hope, while they will employ the full force of reason in rejecting what they find unpalatable."

Every market timer has a set of signals he follows because they worked the last time. The trouble comes when they don't work the next time.

The extrapolation method of forecasting is natural, plausible—and wrong. We feel instinctively that what happened the last time the Fed or the dollar or Congress did this or that will reap the same results if the same stimuli repeat, but they just as often don't, because there are so many other factors impinging on what transpires. As the economist and money manager Henry Kaufman has said, extrapolation may give you the ability to see what's coming down the street but not what's coming around the corner.

Extrapolation is very common among stock analysts. If you studied analysts' forecasts of future earnings, you would find them hard to differentiate from an extrapolation model. Over the short term, moreover, a naive model forecasts just about as well as the professionals do. What is a naive model? One that uses a simple mechanical rule to make a forecast. For instance, one could use a model that predicates that the earnings of a company will change by the

Super Bowl as Crystal Ball

Some years ago, Robert Stovall, a well-known stock market adviser, found a correlation between the Super Bowl winner and the stock market. When the Super Bowl is played each January, the market will close the year higher if the game is won by an "original" NFC team, but decline if the game is won by a team from the now-vanished American Football League. The term "original" means that teams such as Baltimore and Pittsburgh, although now in the American Football Conference, *used* to be in the NFC, and so count as if they were NFC teams. In all of the Super Bowl games played through 1987, the rule had failed only twice, in 1970 and 1984.

The Super Bowl Indicator achieved considerable fame, and is still commented on in the press around game time. Stovall meant it all as a joke, but his spoof caught the public's eye because it's cute, and the number of people interested in the stock market is nowhere near the number who care about the Super Bowl.

The existence of a statistical correlation between two sets of data does not imply any causal link between the two, especially between two games as unrelated as football and stock investing. One must note, however, that because there is no causal link, correlation works just as well in either direction. Why not, then, I decided, use stock market action to predict the winner of the Super Bowl? That way, we could win big bucks in one day, and not have to wait eleven months for the poky old stock market to follow the Super Bowl Indicator.

The Acorn Super Bowl Secret (ASS) is the converse of Stovall's Super Bowl Indicator:

1. If the first five days of January show a gain for the S&P 500, the "original" NFC team will win.

2. If the first five days of January show a loss for the S&P 500, the AFC team will win.

Looking at the twenty-one Super Bowls through 1987, when I undertook my study, the ASS rule predicted the winners with 90 percent accuracy. We had the secret of instant wealth!

So what happened in 1988? The first five days of January were down, so ASS predicted a Denver victory. Instead, Denver got scalped, and our statistician was left looking like a Bronco's ASS.

In the eight years since, though, the indicator has worked remarkably well: the bettor who relied on it would have had six wins, one loss (1994), and one no bet (since the market was flat the first days of 1990). But it could just as easily have gone the other way. I'm afraid the secret of instant wealth remains elusive. The moral for stock market technicians? Statistical correlation without any reasonable causal link between variables is worthless.

same amount as they changed last year. Such a forecast would have no higher degree of error than that of the average half-million-dollar-a-year security analyst.

The extrapolation method of forecasting is natural, plausible—and wrong.

If you are trying to extrapolate growth rates, don't confuse short-term swings with long-term trends. If you are looking at a company in the women's shoe industry as a possible investment, for example, you should expect long-term growth in unit sales of about 2 percent per year. If you find a shoe company with a hot new running shoe, and its sales for the last two years have climbed 15 percent a year, what should you expect in the way of growth over the next five years? Short-term—for another year or two—15 percent might be sustainable, but after that you ought to anticipate reversion to the mean. For the fifth year out, 2 percent growth would be a sensible forecast.

Exceptional growth usually sows the seeds of its own decline. The gaming industry is a naturally attractive business. You fill up a building with slot machines and the public volunteers to come and put money in them for you, and you don't have to provide any product or service in return. When the industry was allowed to expand out of its enclaves in Nevada and Atlantic City, each new casino and riverboat was instantly and gloriously profitable. Harrah's, a winner in this period of expansion, saw its stock go from a 1990 low of 3 to a 1993 high of 40.

Then the free-market system did its work. With profit opportunities as rich as this, who wouldn't build a casino? Competition rose, spread, and squeezed profitability. Harrah's still makes money, but earnings have been considerably lower than forecast, and the stock in late 1996 is selling at only half its 1993 peak.

Competition's progress is predictable. The first casino company in a market needs only one riverboat and a parking lot. The company may even charge an entry fee. Then a second riverboat shows up nearby, and before long there are several. A smart company now has to add expensive amenities: a second boat, access-road improvements, a big parking garage, a hotel, restaurants, a movie complex, and child care are typical expenditures. Competitive pressures eliminate the entry fee, increase advertising outlays, and force more liberal slot machine payoffs. In sum, operating profit margins go down and the investment in the property goes up, until the profitability of gaming goes from high to average.

But in spite of the power of reversion to the mean, in the short term there *is* a certain amount of follow-through, in earnings growth and stock action. There are people who invest on this premise. They are the momentum investors introduced earlier, though "momentum" is a bad metaphor picked up from the physical sciences. Newton discovered that things that have mass have inertia, so that you have to apply force to change their course, and it takes some time to do it. A financial price doesn't have a mass, so price changes can be very, very rapid. You can see a stock that's been doing well suddenly drop 50 percent in a day because of some negative news item. The "momentum" disappears in a flash.

Some studies have indicated that buying last year's best-performing mutual funds works moderately well in the following year, so there is a case for momentum over a few months. The extension of the good performance is probably the result of the fact that the funds' style is in favor. The funds have portfolios that match the way the market happens to want to go at that particular time. They're in the right industries and sectors, and the other funds are not. The trend that's been favorable to the funds' allocation is likely to last another three or four or five quarters, because market trends do persist for a while, whether you call it momentum or something else. You can probably find a statistical correlation that says the strength will go on for a few more quarters. But you can have a statistically significant finding that is still a weak forecasting tool. For the question remains, how long will a trend continue, and when will it reverse? Those are hard questions to answer.

So much of what happens in the market, in the short run, is just random, but that is seldom acknowledged. There has to be a reason the market went or up down yesterday, so *The Wall Street Journal* and the other papers call up analysts and money managers and ask them why. What you usually read in the paper is simply a logical fallacy. Something happened after something else, and therefore the first event must have caused the second event. The bond market goes up a quarter of a point, and a reporter rings up somebody at Salomon Brothers, and the trader she gets on the phone figures his name in the paper would impress his girlfriend, so he looks at his terminal and says, "Well, the Bank of France lowered interest rates yesterday and that had a favorable impact on the U.S. market." So the reporter writes it down, it appears the next morning, and readers nod as though they now understand. The truth is, no one knows why the hell the bond market did what it did.

Most of what happens in the market in the short run is just random noise.

I've been guilty of this foolishness myself when talking to reporters. When the October 1987 market break came, I had been worried about problems in the Persian Gulf. Somebody had fired on an offshore oil platform, and I thought a war might break out. The market fell off for reasons that had nothing to do with the Mideast, but if somebody had called me on the Friday before the crash and asked me why the market was so nervous, I would have pontificated about a war scare.

One might think that with the prowess of computers and the ever greater sophistication of programmers, people could come up with a nearly infallible market-forecasting system. So far, though, it hasn't happened. The systems often fail because, again, of a data-mining issue. The seemingly savvy forecaster's predictive system doesn't work because it didn't really work in the first place; he just had a version of the Super Bowl Indicator.

You have probably heard the story about the market letter writer who sends out 128 free copies of his letter, sixty-four of them recommending that IBM be bought, sixty-four recommending a sale. A month later IBM is down 5 percent, so he throws out the names of the sixty-four people to whom he had recommended buying the stock and works up a second set of letters: thirty-two recommend buying Microsoft, the other thirty-two say it's a sale. This goes on for several weeks until he has eight people who have had four great tips in a row. He then sends them a telegram that says, "Friends, I have just *proved* to you that I am the best forecaster in town. I now have a fifth idea that I am even more sure about than the last four. Your check for only $500 . . ." He's converted a random sequence into a terrific track record.

Mutual fund companies have been suspected of similarly manufacturing performance. If you are a giant management company, you can launch ten start-up funds, seeding each with $100,000. The ten managers agree to only one guideline: that each will do something different from the others. One will buy only high-growth stocks, another only gold stocks, another only Treasury bills—it doesn't matter, as long as they are different. At the end of the year the company's management sees three of the funds have done well, compared to funds in their category. So it cancels the other seven and keeps the three. It's like growing radishes. You thin out the patch. At the end of another two years the company will have one fund with a terrific record. It drops the other two and takes full-page ads in magazines and newspapers for the fund "with the best three-year record in its peer group." Again, you've selected from a random sequence and come up with something that looks valuable.

Is There a Pattern?

Why do we fall for such tricks and listen to market forecasters who are no better than astrologers? Because the human mind is a pattern-seeking mind. We are all descended from people who are good pattern finders, because at some point our ancestors were walking around with some fellow hunters and there was a little rustle in the tall grass a hundred feet ahead. And Og said, "That's the wind," and Magog said, "I think it's a leopard." And Og marched forward and was leopard lunch. Your ancestor is Magog, who read that rustle aright. We're all descended from people who were very good at finding patterns in things.

> Why do we listen to market forecasters who are no better than astrologers? Because the human mind is a pattern-seeking mind.

All of us at some point in our lives lie down on our back on a hillside and look up at the sky and see objects or creatures in the clouds. At least, I hope everyone has done that. If you haven't done it recently, you should borrow a six-year-old girl and go sit on a hill. It's an excellent thing to do. And you will see patterns in the clouds—horses, whales, faces.

You'll see them because we're genetically trained to be pattern recognizers. If you ask a computer scientist what people can do very readily that computers have a tough time doing, the answer will be pattern recognition. You or I could recognize any of thousands of faces instantly. You won't remember all their names, but if you've seen a face before, you'll recognize it. Computers have a very difficult time with pattern recognition. The human brain is itself a very good computer, programmed to perform functions like that. It was damned important to know if that rustle ahead was the wind or a leopard, or if those three men in uniform coming toward you were from your army or theirs.

Beware of False Metaphors

When you stop to think about it, all investing rests on metaphors. Your broker calls you and says, "This is Murray. I've got a stock here that's going to be the next Intel." That's a metaphor. Metaphors are ways of finding common patterns between dissimilar things.

Since they are dissimilar, metaphors and similes require us to consider the degrees of likeness and unlikeness between the things compared. A classic example is "My love is like a red, red rose." That doesn't exactly fit the reality. Your girl is very beautiful, and you love to look at her, but you probably don't mean that she's short, thorny, and lives in your garden.

As essential as metaphors are for investors, therefore, they require critical analysis. In December 1994 the Mexican peso collapsed. The Mexican economy reeled. The Mexican stock market tanked. ("Collapsed," "reeled," and "tanked" are all metaphors, if that's of any interest.)

Investors then sold stocks in Argentina, causing a drop in prices and a run on Argentina's peso. There was no problem with the Argentine economy or banking system. Investors had simply assumed a metaphor: "They speak Spanish and use pesos as money, so they are the same." Never mind that Buenos Aires is 4,609 airline miles away from Mexico. Often those who believe in false metaphors create opportunities for those who think a bit harder.

Bad metaphors trap investors all the time. How often do we read, "This market is just like the market in April 1966"? There are similarities, sure, but not enough to bank on them. Chart reading is a metaphor. Momentum investing is another. In fact, almost all models that forecast the future have to be viewed suspiciously. That is why at Acorn we established a powerful and far-reaching group, the Metaphor Committee, whose ruthless and unsleeping members can pounce at any time, crushing an overworked simile or dismembering a mixed metaphor.

The most complex area in which the committee operates is criticism of mathematical models that predict stock price behavior. It has become popular in recent years to put one's metaphor into a series of equations that can then be run on a computer, adding the veneer of infallibility provided by neatly typed-out rows of numbers.

All models have an inherent limitation on their validity, the Cricket Limit. There is a nearly perfect mathematical fit between air temperature and the pitch at which crickets chirp. As the temperature drops, down to about 50° F., crickets chirp more slowly. One might expect the pitch to decline further as the night cools from

50° to 45°. This doesn't happen; under 50°, the cricket packs it in and stops chirping altogether.

No matter how reliable the relationship of two variables has been (such as interest rates and inflation), there is no reason to think the relationship will hold for previously unknown levels (as happens when inflation rates soar).

In the investment world, however, extrapolating patterns from historical data is unreliable because of the constantly changing nature of that world. We all accept the cliché that the pace of change has accelerated, but I wonder if what that really means has sunk in.

The institutionalization of the market, for example, has had a profound effect on market behavior. Individual investors tend to hold on to their stocks; institutions have been turning over their portfolios almost 100 percent a year. They may not be trying to time the market—many professional managers stay fully invested—but they are constantly changing the names in their portfolios. The incessant stock switching that has taken hold among many professional managers is like a bride's announcing at the wedding reception that she is already planning her divorce. Furthermore, individuals make sales at scattered times, while institutions tend to act in unison. We're back to the herd of zebras, responding similarly to any given stimuli.

This time, the zebras are in a canyon, with the lion asleep at the head wall. Every zebra is going to munch grass right up to the lion's nose, then bolt down the trail just before the lion pounces. Unfortunately, it is a narrow trail, and in fact, the zebras will pile up in a helpless clot at the first narrow point and become instant steak tartare. Many large institutions, responsible for billion-dollar portfolios and dealing in often illiquid markets, claim that they can make a quick switch from stock to stock or stocks to cash, and vice versa. No way. The result is the highly volatile market we have today. It makes very large, very abrupt moves that create impossible situations for timers. By the time they have figured out what's going on, it's already too late.

The incessant stock switching of many professional managers is like a bride's announcing at the wedding reception that she is planning her divorce.

The effect of the globalization of economies and markets—to a degree that far surpasses that of even ten years ago—has had an enormous impact on what happens in our own market. The shift from an industrial to a service economy has also made older data suspect. Wall Street inventions such as program trading and derivatives have introduced new factors that have further muddied the picture. Lately, the influx of hundreds of billions of dollars into mutual funds has tossed in another fresh element.

All those indicators that are supposed to tell you when the bull market is over can, again, be unreliable extrapolations of past behavior. As a prime example, in October 1992 the dividend yield of the S&P 500 fell below 3 percent, and it has been common wisdom that whenever that occurs, the market is ready for a tumble. It always happens, proclaimed the soothsayers (citing 1987 as another instance), and it always will. When the bear didn't pounce, the timers blamed dropping interest rates and rising corporate earnings but declared they were only stalling the inevitable. But still no great correction came, even though the yield stayed under 3 percent. By mid-1996 the dividend yield on the S&P 500 hit a record low of 2.1 percent, while the market was still making new highs.

By that time the pundits had changed their tune. Well, maybe the old signal isn't valid anymore, after all. Now the argument runs: "Investors currently want appreciation more than income, so companies are using their earnings to expand operations or buy back stock, and dividend payouts are going to stay low from now on." (No one has challenged this reasoning, though stocks are increasingly owned by tax-exempt holders who are happy to get dividends, and less by individuals who have to pay taxes on them.) As Wharton professor Jeremy Siegel wrote in his book *Stocks for the Long Run*, "Any yardstick for stock valuation, even one with a sound theoretical basis or one that has worked for more than a century, can stop working."

> Even the timers with the best records have added no return to a buy-and-hold policy. They can claim only that since they are often in cash, they've lowered portfolio volatility.

Meanwhile, a good number of portfolio managers, observing the low dividend yield and other negative signs, moved heavily into bonds and cash, and their performance suffered, in some cases for several years. (One celebrity casualty of the urge to time: Jeff Vinik, late of the Fidelity Magellan fund, who in late 1995 and early 1996 shifted a good part of his portfolio from stocks into bonds, expecting the former to correct and the latter to rally. Wrong on both counts, he was soon no longer employed by Fidelity.) Eventually the Cassandras will prove right—bear markets have not been repealed—but it is very doubtful that the timers will be any better off at the end of the day than if they had just stayed in the stocks of companies they liked. Even the timers with the best records concede that they have added no return to a buy-and-hold policy; their claim is that since they are often in cash, they achieve their returns with lower volatility.

The stock market, at least in the short run, responds to many factors besides profits and dividends. Inflation and interest rates, the supply of new stock underwritings, the money supply, investor confidence, governmental actions, and international events are all factors that interact with one another in subtle, changing, and unpredictable ways. What we have, really, is a complex system with lags and multiple feedback loops.

All such systems share certain characteristics that hinder predictive accuracy. Behavior can be counterintuitive. (A city virtuously builds public housing only to experience an influx of poor rural people that bankrupts the city and trashes the public housing.) The long-term response will often be the opposite of a short-term response. (Price and wage controls bring down the rate of inflation at first but then create distortions that make the situation worse.) Trying to predict what will happen to a complex system by looking at only one part of it leads to inaccurate conclusions. (Trying to predict the market by watching corporate profits alone is a perfect example.) Setting policy to optimize one part of the system often produces poor results for the total system. (Environmental rules to reduce auto exhaust emissions cause large increases in gasoline consumption, so the effect on the total system may be negative.)

The stock market is a reliable indicator of where the economy is headed, but you'll get no help looking at events the other way around.

One might think, for example, that at least the state of the economy would provide a road map to securities prices, but as Peter

Lynch has said, "I spend about fifteen minutes a year on economic analysis. The way you lose money in the stock market is to start off with an economic picture." Market levels simply have little to do with whether the economy is up 3 percent or down 1 percent. They have a great deal to do with cash flow into and out of markets. Every study shows that the stock market is a reliable lead indicator of where the economy is headed, but it's no help trying to look at events the other way around. The economy fluctuates, providing average growth of about 2.5 percent per year in recent times, and, in terms of investment policy, that's about all you can say about it. There is certainly no point in waiting for the economy to grow at a faster rate. You simply have to buy stocks you believe in because you think you've found people who have an important reason to be in business, and then you have to stick with them as long your faith in them remains.

When the market's going down, it's not because you are stupid. And when it's going up, it's not because you are smart.

But nothing seems to stop people from trying to call the market's direction. I sometimes think they are less interested in making money than they are in proving their brilliance. "The market has a will of its own, does it? Very well, I'll tame it and show who's boss." It's a silly challenge. When the market's going down, it's not because you are stupid. And when it's going up, it's not because you are smart.

Bull Market Bewitched

One of the hardest temptations to resist, even for those who don't believe in timing, is the urge to retreat from a bull market that has gone on for a very long time and pushed valuations into ever-higher territory. It seems only common prudence to retire to the sidelines.

During one such recent feverish stretch, I was reading C. S. Lewis's *Chronicles of Narnia* to two of my children, and a chapter in volume six, *The Silver Chair,* struck me as a wonderful metaphor for the seductions of a prolonged bull market. An evil witch, by various magic powders and enchantments, convinces both the adults and children in the tale that her underground world is the only reality and that the real world of the earth and sky, with its sun, moon, and stars, is nothing but a fantasy:

> Then came the Witch's voice, cooing softly like the voice of a wood-pigeon from the high elms in an old garden at three o'clock in the middle of a sleepy, summer afternoon; and it said: "What is the sun that you all speak of? Do you mean anything by the word?"
>
> "Yes, we jolly well do," said Scrubb [one of the children].
>
> "Your sun is a dream . . ." Slowly and gravely the Witch repeated, "There is no sun." And they all said nothing. She repeated, in a softer and deeper voice, "There is no sun." After a pause, and after a struggle in their minds, all four of them said together, "You are right. There is no sun." It was such a relief to give in and say it.

The later stages of a bull market are like that for investors. Some powerful witch coos in our ears, "There is no risk. The market will only go up. Initial public offerings are marvelous. Your stockbroker is your best friend. A limitless, effortless fortune awaits you."

In the Narnia story, our heroes managed to fight off the enchantment at the last moment. The witch changed instantly into her true form, a great loathsome serpent. A prince, handily present—he had also been under her spell—kills her with his sword, and all live happily ever after.

A bull market has the lulling allure of a lovely, soft-voiced woman, but it, too, can become a loathsome beast in an instant. What should you do to foil the market witch in the real world? Once you become aware that you are under a spell, your first reaction is to flee and sell everything. But we know market timing doesn't work. A market may indeed be "overpriced," but it can stay overpriced for years. Bull markets come in all lengths. Your only defense against every sort of market jitters is to think like a long-term investor. If you stare the monster down with focus, patience, and a calm eye, you will be rewarded in the end.

Bull markets come in all lengths.

The Human Factor

Even if one could time the market with sufficient skill to come out ahead of a buy-and-hold strategy, there is another serious consideration: the toll on the human psyche, whether the investor is moving in and out of individual stocks or in and out of mutual funds.

Let's say you are quite good at discerning when the market is over- or undervalued. Only by occasional chance, however, would you be able to call the exact turning points—no one rings a bell, you know—so you have to face weeks and months when you are out of the market while prices are still rising, or in the market when it is still falling. Every day you have to tell yourself that you are right and most investors are wrong. That kind of pressure takes its toll.

Probably the toughest exercise for the timer is deciding, once out, when to get back in. A timer has to be right twice.

Suppose you sell out. The market drops for a few days and you are starting to feel very proud of yourself, when stocks rally sharply and the market is higher than when you left it. You are now in a tough psychological position, because you don't want to admit you made a mistake in getting out and you've now missed part of the move up. If you are a mutual fund manager, I can tell you, you are very uncomfortable. You realize you are now behind your sluggish peers, who just sat there fully invested. You were doing all these clever things, and now they're not working so well. Probably the most common response at that point is to say, "No, I was right and I am still right. This rally is just a trap, to suck in the fools. It'll go up another 2 percent and catch them all. I'm not a fool, so I won't be sucked in." That is a very seductive argument, because it validates your original decision, and it gives you a course of action for the future that labels you wise and sophisticated.

But suppose the market, instead of having sprung a little bull trap and then retreated, continues its rally. The damn fools are still buying! All of a sudden you wake in the middle of the night, sweating over a career crisis. You can say to yourself, "Okay, I was wrong, really wrong. I was wrong the first time, to sell, and I was wrong the second time, not to get back in. I'd better admit I was wrong, get with it, and try to catch up—though I'm so far behind now, I don't know if I *can* catch up." Or you can decide, "No, I'll stay bearish. I'll stay out of the market a while longer. It *has* to go down soon . . . doesn't it?" But you feel very, very nervous making that decision. You are really caught between two impossible choices. And as a mutual fund manager, you know you are going to be in deep trouble for a very long time if performance lags; your career may never recover.

You have probably read that a big part of bull market moves occurs in the first few weeks of those moves. In 1991, for example, when the S&P 500 rose 30.5 percent, more than half of that climb came in the twenty-two trading days following January 16, the day the Gulf War started. Another 7.8 percent of the rise came in just the last six trading days of the year.

Bull market returns are highly concentrated. A University of Michigan study showed that the market's ninety best trading days between 1969 and 1993—barely 1 percent of that period—accounted for 95 percent of the market's gains. Another, even longer-term study showed that if you, in your timing efforts, were out of the market a critical 7 percent of the 780 months from 1926 through 1990 you would have earned absolutely nothing from sixty-four years of investing.

No mutual fund manager who relies on market timing has kept his job for fifteen years.

I believe the should-I-or-shouldn't-I dilemma eventually nailed every market timer who's tried to be in the mutual fund business. No mutual fund manager who relies on market timing has kept his job for fifteen years.

Individual investors who try to time the market will be tossed on the same horns. Trying to be a timer is a great way to make yourself a nervous wreck. Few people are built to be traders. But I think it's even tougher on professional money managers who try to be timers. The psychological pressure is greater. An individual investor can do as he or she pleases. If he wants to own bonds instead of stocks, or buy a boat instead of owning either stocks or bonds, nobody is going to say, "You're not doing it right. You're fired." Your family may grumble if you get it wrong, but the reason you're running the money is that they think you know more about investments than they do, so they'll probably say, "Well, you were just being conservative." The professional, on the other hand, has his or her career—and self-esteem—on the line. There's a bit of a difference between missing a putt on Sunday with the boys, when it's going to cost you $3, and missing the putt on TV in a PGA match, when it will cost you $250,000.

One at a Time

Whatever the reasons, it has proved just about impossible to predict the market with enough accuracy and consistency to make money out of the process. A lot of people who have developed series of indicators that worked well in the past try to convince us otherwise. Their forecasts can work for a time, and then they don't. Even the hottest gurus last only two years, at most three. How many called the 1987 break and stayed bearish for the next five years? Time after time certain people get reputations as being clever, and that lasts until the next time. Do you remember when the press hung on every word of the oracles Joseph Granville and, later, Robert Prechter? Their ability to call market turns was uncanny—until, not so uncannily, they failed. As Cicero said to the Roman Senate: "It seems to me that no soothsayer should be able to look at another soothsayer without laughing."

I truly believe, then, that one is better off spending his time finding good stocks and mutual funds and holding on to them for the long pull. Yes, that means ignoring the daily pronouncements about where interest rates, the bond market, and stocks are headed. Certainly in the dozen years up to the day I am writing this book, anytime you held cash for any period longer than a few weeks or a few months, it's been a mistake. Besides, even when "corrections" last several years, the market always goes on to new highs. So the naive optimist who stays fully invested will drive a Mercedes when he retires, while the intelligent pessimist, who can always pull out a long list of devastating problems facing the country and the economy, will have to be satisfied with his seven-year-old Chevy.

Businesses, too, have their cycles, but these are easier to see and react to than economic or market cycles. Somebody who comes up with a terrific line of athletic shoes will have a wonderful two or three, maybe four years, but you know that sooner or later somebody else is going to come up with a better shoe or people are going to decide they don't want to wear anything that looks like an athletic shoe. You have a far better chance of figuring out when to get out of that stock than you do of calling market turns. Your focus, then, should be on one stock at a time, or one group of stocks. That's what you hope your mutual fund manager is good at—not calling the next 100 points up or down.

No soothsayer should be able to look at another without laughing.

Any stock can sell at a high or low price relative to its "true value," assuming there is such a thing as a central or true value, an article of faith that all certified financial analysts are expected to uphold—though no one has ever seen it. You will see a central value about the time you see an angel. But I still believe it's easier to get a handle on when a stock gets overdone than when the market as a whole has become too pricey.

My philosophy is just to keep looking at our stocks, one by one. If one we own seems more attractive than the others, then we put more money into it. If it's less attractive, we sell it and put the money into other names. New candidates for purchase are evaluated the same way. It's laborious and, as I've noted, not particularly glamorous. But it's a doable job. And it works.

If you don't find enough attractive stocks, the cash accumulates, as a residual. That's very different from the operation of the market timer, who says, "I want to have 32 percent cash by the end of the week, and I will sell stocks to make that happen." When you look at stocks one a time, the cash is just what's left over at the end of the day, and you don't worry about it too much. That, I think, makes a lot more sense than scrutinizing entrails.

10

//

LIVING THROUGH THE CRASH

When the market jumped off a cliff on October 19, 1987—508 points in one day—I don't mind admitting I was shaken. What we had made in a year we lost in a week. It was like being in a car crash and waking up in the hospital and finding you'd lost a leg. You can't believe what's happened to you.

After the first tremors, on Friday, the sixteenth, I felt we were in for something very big, disturbing, and important, and I decided to keep a diary, hour by hour, of what was transpiring. When you live through a catastrophic event, whether it be a stock market collapse or other business or personal calamity, you have a lot of reactions at the time that soon blur in your memory. When you think about the situation a year later, you have sanitized those reactions. You are too likely to come up with a version in which you understood immediately what was going on and took all the right actions, calmly and heroically. The truth is, you were suffering the same feelings of panic and irresolution as everyone else.

As the market teetered, I wanted to capture the sense of what was happening as it happened. The idea of keeping the diary came from a then recently published book, George Soros's *The Alchemy of Finance*. The fabled hedge fund manager had recorded his thoughts about the gyrations of currencies, stocks, and bonds during the period from August 1985 through November 1988, just to give people a glimpse into the thought processes of a master of what is called macroinvesting. His account tells us how someone who makes decisions makes decisions. George is pretty smart, I reasoned. If a diary worked for him, it would work for me. The following is a distillation of what I jotted down during five critical, unnerving days.

Friday, October 16

I was cheerful this morning. The market has been weak for seven weeks. The severe drop in September, a frequent seasonal event, might have been enough to wash out much of the overpricing in stock prices. Acorn has been outperforming the S&P 500 since the August 25 high, as the blue chips dropped much faster than the smaller companies. The Acorn portfolio was in a strong position to resist a decline, with 12 percent in U.S. and Japanese short-term paper, and 16 percent in Asian and European stocks. Many careful studies have shown that foreign stock markets are only moderately correlated with the U.S. market, and this has been true so far today, with most Asian markets at new highs, ignoring the weak U.S. market. In addition, Acorn is short 90 S&P 500 Index Futures and carries a thus-far-profitable 80-unit straddle—long 80 Value Line Index Futures/short 80 S&P 500 Futures.

My cheerfulness didn't last. By afternoon, the market was telling a powerful message. Stocks were in a severe decline on enormous volume. Index futures pricing was erratic; the December futures should sell about two points higher than the index itself under equilibrium conditions, but during much of the day futures were at discounts to the index, making trading difficult. At the close, the market had set a new volume record—343 million shares—and a record drop of 15.14 on the S&P 500, a 5.1 percent decline. Acorn was off only 1.7 percent, so, relative to the market, we did very well. The situation required action; I put in sell orders on seven foreign stock positions, figuring it was time to take profits and move the money back to the U.S. market.

Monday, October 19

The news from the Persian Gulf was ominous, with Iran firing a missile into a Kuwaiti oil installation. The market news from Japan, Hong Kong, and Europe was terrifying even before the New York market opened. Only about a quarter of my foreign sell orders had been executed. All of the markets in the world had record down days as the New York decline spread a deadly cloud of panic around the world. Hong Kong couldn't make it; the exchange was closed down Monday night. [It wouldn't reopen for the rest of the week.] It was obvious that the panic cloud was going to come back around from Europe and get us again.

I resolved to be active in this panicky situation, knowing that many stocks would trade at throwaway prices. I called in Chuck McQuaid, Terry Hogan, and Leah Zell, the three Acorn analysts, and told them to take all of their work in process on new ideas and put it aside until further notice. Instead, each was asked for the names of four or five favorite companies, regardless of price. Price would come to us, I figured. This wish list became the center of my decision process, accompanied by sell orders in a number of current holdings.

The market decline was prodigious. Foreign buyers had turned into sellers. Mutual fund managers were forced to dump stocks to meet redemptions as their shareholders changed from careful investors into a lynch mob. Portfolio insurance managers put in sell orders on index futures, causing their prices to fall to unprecedented discounts relative to the underlying stock values. In turn, program traders sold stock to capture the spread, forcing the market down further. Many of the hedges could not be executed on the floor, so that the hedging techniques proved unusable when most needed. The volume was so heavy that prices on the Quotrons were an hour or more delayed, adding more uncertainty to a situation that already had a bucketful. The emotional feeling was like the wild adrenaline high you would get on a racing sailboat hit by a sudden thunderstorm. At the end of the day, Acorn had bought $6 million of stock and sold $3 million worth on twenty-two trades, a record level for the fund. Our futures position made $4.4 million in the day. The fund was down 8 percent, another record, but the S&P 500 dropped an astonishing 20 percent, so by comparison we appeared to be in great shape.

Tuesday, October 20

The wild sailing continued today. David Hale of Kemper claimed that computers were jumping out of the windows in Chicago and New York. Our trading was even heavier than on Monday, $8 million of buys and an equal value of sells, involving twenty different stocks. Our wish list was doing its job, guiding us to a buy of forty thousand Cray Research at 48, down from 85 in two days. Cray was back to 73 a few hours later. The market took off in a strong rally, but to my dismay, only in the blue chips. Many over-the-counter stocks had been locked out of trading on Monday and were collapsing on Tuesday as a catch-up move. The S&P 500 closed up 5 percent, but Acorn, like the Value Line Index, was down 7 percent, reversing all of the relative gain of Monday.

Wednesday, October 21

The rally continued, with the S&P 500 rising a record 21.51 points. Acorn went up, but a lot less than the market. Emotionally, the two-day adrenaline rush was over. I was exhausted and upset. The last three days felt like a month. Our trading was still very active. I had bought futures to cover our short position late yesterday—not very well timed—but resold them in the afternoon at an excellent profit. The rally looked as tired as I was.

Thursday, October 22

The rally was over. The market started down in the morning, with delayed openings on many key stocks. I sold some more futures. The market closed down 4 percent, on nearly 400 million shares. By this week's standards, a quiet day.

After the Shock

For the five trading days Friday to Thursday, the S&P 500 and Acorn both went down 17 percent, with no sign that the drop was over. Some things had worked. Net redemptions for the week were only

100,000 shares. Our futures positions produced a $4.4 million profit. We were able to buy and sell record amounts of stock, adding value in the process. The crucial negative surprises were, of course, the size and speed of the decline, and the immediate collapse of the foreign markets.

On the way to lunch on Tuesday, I was walking with two of my associates. "Tell me," I asked, "what is that big bright thing in the sky?" They looked confused but figured out that it was the sun. "The same sun that was there last week?" I continued. They agreed it was. "Then maybe the world hasn't changed so much just because stocks went down," I concluded.

However philosophical that final note in my diary, I was worried that *our* world had indeed changed. I was afraid we'd only seen the overture to a long and nasty bear market, maybe to a severe economic depression. Over the long run, the stock market reflects what happens in the real world. Sometimes it signals what's happening when the pattern of actual events isn't yet clear. And sometimes, too, it rings a bell about what's ahead.

When, in my concern, I tried to raise cash, I found that there were no buyers for most of my small-company stocks. And as the diary makes clear, when I tried to sell some foreign issues, that was no use either: all the markets tanked. That wasn't supposed to happen. Diversification across borders, we'd been assured, would dampen total portfolio volatility, but everyone around the world got mashed. So much for academic theory.

In scrounging for whatever cash I could get my hands on, I used the carpenter system. That's when you look for the nails that are sticking up and bash them. I sold whatever stocks had held up relatively well.

I needn't have been so apprehensive, of course. Within months the market made up its loss and went on to new highs. I sold some fine stocks I should have held. But at least I bought others, often at ridiculous prices. Bear markets are weird: you can buy the best of stocks dirt cheap.

On the whole, I'd probably have been as well off if I'd stood pat in 1987, instead of selling in something of a panic, only to grab other stocks that looked too cheap to pass up. But at the time stoic firmness didn't necessarily seem like the best response. What was happening was very, very frightening, and when you're that frightened, it's hard to tell calmness from paralysis. I just felt I had to do *something*. When a stock was 40 on Monday and it's 22 on Tuesday, you can't just stand there.

Some market commentators say that 1987 taught a bad lesson. Too many people, seeing the market right itself so rapidly after its fall, concluded that all breaks are quickly healed. They don't understand that some bear markets last for years.

But I think the lesson was probably a healthy one. Very dramatic events like October 1987, or even extended stretches of low returns, don't mean a great deal in the long run. Anyway, you can't predict when the bad times are coming. How many pundits were wailing at the end of 1994 that the market was too high and poised for another October 1987? Then the Dow Industrials proceeded to skyrocket 37 percent in 1995 and another 29 percent in 1996. You can't predict how long the bad times will last either. So you might just as well stay invested.

The October 1987 crash made heroes of some timers who had been crying out warnings. Most of them failed to get back in, and their names are now forgotten.

The October crash made heroes of some timers who had been crying out warnings during the summer and early fall. But most of them failed to get back in, and their names are now forgotten. I know of several investors with considerable portfolios who were so terrified by the 1987 break that they used the subsequent rally to bail out of the market and have wanted no part of it ever since. They have missed out on one of the most sustained rewarding periods in market history. Once again, it seems, the lesson was that timing doesn't work. You just have to hang in there.

An Earlier Episode

The excruciating bear market of 1973–74 was very different, but its lessons were similar. It was a strange bear market. I went back and checked recently and found no day in 1973 when the market dropped by as much as 2 percent, the very opposite of what happened in the terrible days of October 1987. The market just slowly and steadily eroded. And it looked as if it was bottoming out in the fall of 1973, but then the Yom Kippur War broke out and OPEC slapped its oil embargo on the United States.*

OPEC's action caused a world recession in 1974, and the market, which had seemed to be recovering its health, headed down again, and this time it was much more volatile. It's almost as though we had two bear markets, one right after the other. But the total effect was brutal. The net asset value of a share of Acorn at the end of the second quarter of 1970 was $7.54. More than four years later, at the end of the third quarter of 1974, it had dropped to $6.19.

One lesson 1973–74 taught us, repeated in 1987, is that bear markets are great times to load up on stocks. In the third quarter of 1974, when the market was reaching its bottom, the weighted average price-earnings ratio of the Acorn portfolio was a mere 4.3 times estimated 1974 earnings. Stocks don't get cheaper than that. But when pessimism reigns, nobody cares. Which evokes the same

---

*President Carter wrongly reacted by putting a lot of extremely foolish regulations into effect that turned a problem into a crisis. Market forces are very good at sending gasoline from places that have too much to places that have too little. When the government took over the assignment and directed gasoline stocks to designated locations, we all ended up waiting in line for an hour or more to fill our tanks. When Carter removed the regulations, the lines vanished within twenty-four hours.

zebra-lion metaphor. After the second quarter of 1974, I wrote my shareholders: "Unless an investor believes that 'the end of the world' is coming soon, one should be eager to own stocks at today's low prices." We were just three months from the bottom. A good call, no doubt a lucky call. I don't believe in timing. I do believe in buying what's cheap.

Bear markets are great times to load up on stocks. I don't believe in timing. I do believe in buying what's cheap.

The second lesson I took away from the seventies is that even in bad times for the economy, the real recessions, you can find opportunities if you think about things hard enough. The oil embargo slammed the economy, but it made looking for oil and gas far more profitable. When the price of oil went from $3 a barrel to $9 a barrel, energy company profits took off. We saw a theme staring at us. We invested heavily in crude oil and natural gas producers Houston Oil—which, as we've already seen, proved one of my all-time biggest winners—Ranger Oil, and Pan Ocean, and drilling contractors Rowan and Dearborn-Storm. What's more, to exploit the drive to expand alternative energy sources, especially coal, we bought Riley and Mine Safety Appliances. At the end of the third quarter of 1973, these seven stocks accounted for a third of the Acorn portfolio, and they made a lot of money for us.

Which brings up another point. Market timers usually say their big service to mankind is to keep investors on the sidelines, smug and happy, in nasty bear markets. They love to dwell on bear markets. They relish, for example, pointing to the fact that the Dow touched 1000 in 1966 and didn't rise above it for good until late 1982. That sounds as though investors made no money for sixteen years. Some probably didn't, but we did at the fund, and the oil stocks were a big reason. A flat market doesn't mean you can't find stocks that go up.

A flat market doesn't mean you can't find stocks that go up.

From a professional's point of view, as a matter of fact, sideways markets are a pretty good time. If the market is collapsing, which stocks you pick is almost irrelevant. The same is true in a runaway bull market. You don't need to be an analyst. The best investors then are kids who have never lived through a bear market and who just heedlessly buy whatever's moving. In a relatively flat, quiet market, on the other hand, company judgments pay off. The good companies do a little better and the bad companies do a little worse. We earn our keep.

The Crash of 1637

If you want to study crashes, why not start with the first one? The Great Tulip Mania of 1635–37 is a classic example of a boom followed by the inevitable and swift collapse. I suggest the account in Simon Schama's *The Embarrassment of Riches: An Interpretation of Dutch Culture in the Golden Age*, a marvelous evocation of seventeenth-century Holland.

The Tulip Mania shared some common characteristics with other speculative cycles:

1. The country had grown prosperous in the preceding decade, creating investable funds. Holland was the richest country in Europe in 1635.

2. The fundamentals behind the speculation held a kernel of real value and growth potential. Tulips were an exotic and valuable flower in Europe in the early seventeenth century. Bulbs were in demand, especially for new and flamboyant varieties.

3. The market rose at a moderate rate for many years, creating good profits for the professionals, including Dutch tulip farmers. After a while, the public entered the market and the rate of price gains rapidly increased.

4. The upswing took many months to build. As prices continued to climb, enthusiasm increased, and speculative prices soon lost contact with the real world. At the end of 1636, a pound of tulip bulbs sold for a year's income for a middle-class family.

5. The collapse was very abrupt, wiping out the entire bull phase in a couple of days.

6. The government intervened after the crash to try to sort things out. In Holland, all of the trades of the four precrash months were canceled. Only a nominal payment by the buyer to the seller was required by the courts.

The seventeenth century didn't see the last speculation in flowers. In 1984, I invested in Melridge, a grower of lily bulbs, at about $10 a share. Two years later, I sold, having doubled my money. The stock kept climbing, reaching 39 that year. In 1987, it was revealed that Melridge had made a series of fraudulent transactions with its Dutch subsidiary, and it filed for bankruptcy. The stock was soon worthless.

Thinking About Risk

To gain a perspective on bear markets, it might help to look at them in terms the academics have provided.

We've probably all heard about "beta." Professor William Sharpe, who shared the Nobel Prize for Economics in 1990, pioneered its invention as a way to measure the risk of stock portfolios. Risk is defined as volatility. Portfolio risk (beta) is the amount the portfolio will move in response to a market move. The Acorn Fund, for example, has a beta of about 0.9, which means if the stock market moves 20 percent in either direction, Acorn ought to move about 18 percent.

The concept of beta as a measure of risk and potential return—since the more risk you take, the more you should expect to make—has been under attack of late, but on the whole I think it is still a useful tool. It gives you an idea of how much you can expect the value of your portfolio to bounce around. If you won't need your money for twenty years, you might not care much, but if you think you might need it in two years, you'd better worry about the volatility of your portfolio. The easiest way to change the beta of a portfolio is by changing the ratio between cash and stocks, since cash has a beta of zero.

Sharpe also had a big hand in developing the Capital Asset Pricing Model, which says the expected return of a portfolio that tracks the market is the sum of two parts. The first is the "risk-free" rate, which is usually stated as the Treasury bill rate. The second is a "risk premium" that measures the amount of extra return investors expect in order to take the risk of owning stocks. The size of the risk premium, a measure of investors' confidence, or what Keynes called their "animal spirits," varies.

This concept gives us a way to measure bull and bear markets. In a bull market, people speculate on a rosy future, so they settle for a low risk premium, sometimes even a below-zero risk premium. After all, they reason, the market is bound to go up, so it's not really risky. In a bear market, euphoria switches to fear; everyone fears a recession or even a financial panic, or perhaps a war. The financial measure of this fear is the increase in the required risk premium before investors will part with their money.

"Buy low, sell high." Fine, but what does "buy low" mean? The answer is, you buy low when the risk premium is high, and you sell high when the risk premium is low. On further reflection, of course, this does not solve the problem, but only restates it. Future risk premiums are no easier to forecast than anything else.

Pessimistic forecasts are rampant in bear markets, of course, but even in the best of times there are always problems out there. The economy's humming, but we could be turning toward a recession by the end of the year. Inflation looks as if it could reignite. The dollar is weak. The balance of payments is terrible; the federal budget a joke. Corporations and consumers are awash in debt. The banks or real estate or some other important sector is in deep trouble. A crisis looms somewhere in the world. There's always a list.

In bleak periods falling stock prices are not part of the problem. They are part of the solution.

As a bull market gathers steam, investors pay less and less attention to the problems and more attention to the opportunities. And vice versa in bear episodes. It is important to remember at the bleak times that falling stock prices are not part of the problem, but part of the solution. We all want to buy stocks when the risk premium is high and sell when the risk premium is low.

Seat Belts Fastened?

Will there be another trauma time like 1973–74, when the market lost nearly half its value, or another day like October 19, 1987? I don't know. But I do know there will be bear markets, for as we discovered earlier, trees don't grow to the sky. I just don't know when they will happen, how bad they will be, or how long they will last.

But there are plenty of people who think they do know. They write books about why we are poised on the brink of doom and why, within months, another 1929—forget 1973–74 or 1987!—awaits us.

If you look at a shelf of market-wisdom books of the last quarter century—of which this is going to be number 685—you find that a large number of them, and some of the most successful, have been those predicting imminent disaster. Harry Browne's *You Can Profit from a Monetary Crisis* reached number one on the *New York Times* best-seller list in 1974. Douglas Casey's *Crisis Investing* was on the list for twenty-nine weeks in 1979. Ravi Batra's *The Great Depression of 1990* (now there was a great call!) stayed on the list for much of 1988. My favorite title, though, was *Blood in the Streets: Investment Profits in a World Gone Mad*, by J. D. Davidson and Sir William Rees-Mogg, which Summit Books published in 1987.* They all predicted doomsdays that never arrived.

People seem to get a lot of joy out of contemplating disasters. They provide a thrill. Suppose someone came to Steven Spielberg and said, "I want to do a movie about life in a shipyard. The workers are building a great ship, and I will capture their tireless efforts—drawing the plans, fabricating the components, welding the steel, laying the keel—putting together this great behemoth day by day by day." Sound like fun? "Hell, no!" the average moviegoer would say. "Sounds boring to me."

---

*Actually, the book made some very astute calls: "The Soviet Union will inevitably break apart" (page 143); "Six deadly storm clouds are gathering over real estate" (page 273); "We predict that hundreds of S&Ls will go broke" (page 290).

Steven Spielberg doesn't want to do that movie. But a second agent comes along who says, "This is going to be a movie about the sinking of a great ocean liner. It hits an iceberg and starts to sink, and we'll see everybody running around in a panic and doing incredibly heroic and romantic things in the face of overwhelming danger." Everybody will say, "Great! I want to see that movie. I want to see it twice."

Disasters and tragedies and explosions and wars are much more interesting than hard work and building ships and factories and skyscrapers. Earthquakes are more dramatic than civil engineering.

So predictions of economic collapse sell more books. They sound very sophisticated, too, because they are filled with these impressive reasons why another 1929 is inevitable. The authors' explanations sound very logical and compelling. Optimists aren't compelling. They don't have a lot to say. And they sound naive. "Why are you optimistic?" "Well, things aren't so bad. On the whole, the world's getting better. People are working and building their companies. They're getting along and it will be all right." Who wants to buy a book that says, "Don't worry, be happy"?

No, the audience wants the thrill of impending doom. "Who knows?" everyone thinks. "Maybe these people will prove right." Bad things certainly happen with enough frequency in this world. As a friend of mine likes to say, "There are people dying today who have never died before."

But even though bad things happen to companies, industries, even the economy as a whole for a time, somehow society as a whole still moves forward. Problems usually get solved. Recessions end. Somehow the country stumbles on and companies continue to make a profit. If you don't need to put your hands on your money for a few years, I'd say stocks are still the best place to keep it.

11

WHILE YOU'RE AT IT, INCLUDE THE WORLD

Five hundred years after Columbus discovered America, American investors have discovered the world.

Just thirty years ago, from a U.S. investor's point of view, the rest of the world did not exist. Or at least it could be totally ignored, for it was wholly irrelevant.

Asian and Latin American markets were so small as to be inconsequential. And Europe was growing more slowly than the United States, so why bother with her? There was nothing you could do over there that you couldn't do better here at home. If you wanted something exotic in your portfolio, you could buy some Royal Dutch Shell or Unilever, but you realized no advantage over Exxon or Procter & Gamble. Occasionally I would pick up a foreign stock—I bought Komatsu, a Japanese manufacturer of construction equipment, as early as 1970—but I didn't get serious about internationalizing the portfolio until about a decade ago. And I was earlier than most.

Also, the dollar was the only real money back then. There was the dollar and Monopoly money, and that was it. Remember when you took your vacations in Italy because everything was so cheap? You had a wonderful dinner for 18,000 lire, and you laughed at those foolish Italians who didn't even know how to have real money. Eighteen thousand lire sounded like a lot, but it came out to $7.20. Those were terrific times for Americans, but they're gone forever.

Today, of course, investors accept the fact that the United States is one country among many, the dollar is one currency among many, and the U.S. stock market is one stock market among many. Ours may still be the largest market—though for a short spell in the late 1980s the Japanese market, ridiculously inflated, was bigger in total capitalization terms—but we sure as heck aren't the only one.

Somewhere back in the sixties and seventies, Europe began to get its act together, Japan became a powerhouse, and Southeast Asia began filling up with bustling workshops, so that Korea, Taiwan, Hong Kong, Singapore, Malaysia, and Indonesia turned into important manufacturing centers. About 1985 I realized that many of the U.S. companies I owned were getting their asses kicked by some hustler in Hong Kong who was turning out a quality rival product at a lower price. I started hearing all kinds of stories from my companies: "We had to close down our factory in Kentucky because somebody's bringing up stuff from Guatemala that we can't compete with."

As a Chicago Cubs fan, I had long realized you can love losers, but it is not a wise idea to bet on them. (I don't know why people worry about the Cubs. As some sage has noted, anybody can have a bad century once in a while.)

Bet on good companies regardless of what country they're domiciled in.

I figured we had better start looking at some of these foreign companies. My motto became "Don't bitch; switch."

I told my staff that we would find winners wherever domiciled and bet on them, because that's what we're supposed to do in this business. Ignore patriotism and sentiment, I fearlessly declared, and find out where the growing companies are, and if it's an electric motor manufacturer in Hong Kong or a machine tool maker in Germany, that's where the money will go.

Free Markets Triumph

Then came one of the supreme upheavals of the century: the destruction of the idea of state control over economic events. Until the past decade half the world was owned by the Communist monoliths, the Soviet Union and China. Communism was a laboratory experiment to see if totalitarian controls could alter human nature. After seventy years, the experiment was ruled a failure. Whether it was the Soviet model, the Chinese model, the Hungarian model, the Vietnamese model, or the Cuban model, they all ended in complete and utter chaos, leaving impoverished populations and worthless industries. After all those years of Communist fiddling, the Polish government couldn't figure out a way to let a man walk into a pub and buy a cheese sandwich and a glass of beer.

Government control of the economy in India was almost as thorough, though it took a slightly different format. Europe was more socialist than not. Even the United States had overregulated many of its industries. In Latin America excessive regulation, stupid taxation policies, and government ownership of major industries had kept the growth rate in the cellar for most of the last fifty years. Africa, then as now, was struggling to find an identity.

Then, almost overnight, came a marvelous transformation. I don't know of any empire in history that collapsed as fast as the Soviet Union did, not even the empire of the Mongols in the fourteenth century, when Genghis Khan's great-grandson packed it in. The Soviet Union just popped like a balloon. Eastern Europe, too, was free. And China changed into whatever the hell it is, an ostensibly Communist state with dozens of Chinese companies lining up to do public offerings in the West with the hope of one day being listed on the New York Stock Exchange. Whatever you call it, it ain't Mao Tse-tung.

Western Europe has been kept busy privatizing. With Great Britain leading the way, countries have been selling off their steel companies and phone companies and gasworks and insurance companies and big banks—not necessarily because they became born-again capitalists, but because those enterprises were so bureaucratic and inefficient they were breaking the national budgets. At the same time, some Latin American countries have gone from backward, problem areas to exemplars of high growth.

The entire world, in short, unwound all the changes that had started in 1917, when all the clever folks were high on socialism, determined to put more and more economic decisions under state control. Mankind made a complete swing in the other direction, releasing enormous amounts of energy.

Nice things are happening as a result. We don't have to worry nearly as much about being blown up by an atomic bomb. Instead of being targets for nuclear missiles, China and Russia have become targets for venture capital. A great many people who have been living in very deprived circumstances are going to live much fuller, more pleasant lives.

We have some new risks as a result, it is true. The risk of small wars has probably increased, because you no longer have dictators to say, "Cool it, guys." So Yugoslavia dissolved into war, and parts of the old Soviet Union announced their readiness to fight for their own sovereignty. I wonder if Iraq would have attacked Kuwait in 1990 if a strong Soviet influence had still been around to say, "We don't think you ought to do this, and we won't support you if you go ahead with it." With Soviet sponsorship gone, the Iraqis realized their weapons systems were going to deteriorate, and if they were going to do anything militarily, they had to do it soon. So we had a major world crisis.

Another resultant problem is that we now have a world capital shortage. All those decades of Communist and socialist control took their toll. Russia and China and India maintained large military forces and neglected everything else. To travel through Eastern Europe or Russia is to witness an appalling urban and industrial landscape. Housing is deplorable; hundreds of millions live in hovels. Go through the industrial plants and you find antiquated machinery that is basically useless. And so are the products they turn out. (We are told that production rates have fallen in Russia, but the statistics are meaningless; under communism the factories may have been turning out more goods, but they were so shoddy—badly designed and badly made—that they had no real value.) Pollution is a horrible problem. Russian oil pipelines leak, causing frequent fires, explosions, and soil pollution. Seventy years of communism was like five years of total war in terms of physical destruction.

Those who have the capital can ask a high price for it.

So these countries, as in the aftermath of every war, need everything—food, roads, industrial plant, housing. That has created an enormous demand for capital, and those who have the capital can therefore ask a high price for it. That keeps interest rates high—and stock prices low, because the Russian and Polish and Chinese enterprises looking for financing are risky, and investors say, "Sorry, but you can't expect me to pay fifteen or twenty times earnings for very-high-risk companies. Eight or nine times earnings for these businesses is about right."

The Rush to Buy Foreign

It is truly marvelous the way U.S. investors, seeing all these benef-
icent events in the world, decided all at once that international investing was the thing to do. Up until 1993, about 5 percent of the
cash flow from investors, both individuals and institutions, was
heading outside the United States. But in 1993 the money ear-
marked for international funds jumped from 5 percent of the total
to 50 percent. I don't know why the percentage went from 5 percent to 50 percent instead of from 5 percent to 14 percent or some
other more likely number, but it happened—the most dramatic
shift in market-share preference that I have ever seen. By the fall of
1993, $4 billion a month was pouring into international funds. At
the same time institutions were increasing their overseas holdings,
though not as overwhelmingly. Suddenly, everyone seems to have
realized that Malaysia and Hungary and all the rest of the once-
ignored nations were shouting, "Hey, we need your money and
we'll pay you more for it than you can get at home." People over-
did it in 1993, as usually happens, and 1994 was a down year for
foreign stocks, with 1995 and 1996 only modestly better.

Americans underown foreign stocks.

There's no stopping the tide now. I agree with those who say that
in a few years U.S. investors will have 15 or 20 percent of their investments in non-U.S. companies (it's about 8 percent now).
What's more, I believe that 20 percent is too small an allocation. I
think a third would be more like it, maybe even 50 percent.

One reason for the new willingness to entrust money to overseas investments is that the hunger and competition for American capital are keen enough to have convinced country after country to adopt investor-friendly policies. Many countries have loosened or abandoned the limits on how much stock can be owned by foreigners. Exchanges are adopting stricter, more reliable standards. Regulatory agencies are being given real power, including the authority to crack down on insider trading. (Some insider trading rules have actually been enforced!) Prices in most markets are now easy to get on quote machines. Clearing and settling trades are faster and less error-prone. News disclosures and earnings reports have become more timely; the secretiveness that prevailed is quickly giving way to what those in the business call "transparency." Finally, accounting standards are improving.

Germany has been a notoriously difficult market because of its opaque accounting practices. Management's attitude toward investors seems to have been, "Our business is none of your business." But the German establishment finally decided that opening its books could reduce its cost of capital. In 1993 Daimler-Benz decided to list its stock on the New York Stock Exchange, with all of the disclosure requirements that entails. And the German government is taking measures to make investment generally more attractive: reform of a tax system that has favored private over publicly traded companies, the passage of insider trading laws, and simplification of capital structures that, for example, restricted voting shares to nationals.

The rest of the world hasn't quite caught up with the United States yet, but give it time. After all, our present system didn't spring into being full-blown either. A look at the 150-to-200-year history of the U.S. stock market will show that it took a long time to develop shareholder rights, investor communications, protections against stock manipulations, and all the rest. At least overseas exchanges have a model to emulate.

One by-product of the outflow to foreign stocks may not have been faced squarely: it can cause some weakness in the U.S. market. If I invest money in Jakarta, I don't invest it in Peoria. When cash flow into the U.S. market is diminished, it hurts stock prices. In addition, when the company in Jakarta uses the new capital to turn itself into an important producer and exporter, U.S. companies will feel the competition. On the other hand, we're also creating new consumer and industrial markets, which should benefit our exporting companies. If that Jakarta firm builds new factories, that ought to be great news for construction equipment makers like Caterpillar.

World market rules are catching up with the United States—slowly.

In short, U.S. companies are going to be both helped and hurt by these trends, which only underscores the need for today's investors to think globally. Most European investors have thought globally all along, because the stock buyer in, say, Brussels knows that the Belgian economy alone doesn't offer enough opportunities for his money. The U.S. investor, too, is learning that parochialism is hobbling.

At Acorn, we found a company in Malaysia called Genting. Gambling is a good business, but competition can be a problem, as we have discussed. How much better to have a monopoly! Genting not only serves a population of fervent Southeast Asian gamblers, but it runs the only casino within a thousand miles. Then we thought, if the gambling business is going to do so well worldwide, why not buy the company that makes slot machines? That led us to International Game Technology and some U.S. gaming stocks.

These days the country where a company's headquarters hap-

pens to be domiciled is often more or less irrelevant. If a Swedish company exports 90 percent of what it makes and 35 percent of those goods are sold in the United States and 25 percent in Japan, is it really a Swedish stock? We assign each company to a country, but the assignment is often arbitrary.

Buy American?

Some investors insist that it is still best to stick to U.S. companies, where you can count on full disclosure, protective regulation, no currency hedging questions, and plenty of Wall Street research. By owning multinational companies, they further argue, you can still reap the harvest of growing economies abroad.

In answer, I would say first that diversifying away from the U.S. dollar is probably valuable in itself. You don't want all your money in one stock, or in one industry, and I'm not sure you want all your money in one currency. That's particularly true in light of the debt trap this country has got itself into and what that portends for the economy and the dollar. Over the last couple of decades the U.S. debt-to-GDP ratio has gone from 25 percent to 55 percent, and I am one of those who believe this puts us on a straight line to disaster. Interest payments on our national debt eat so much of the budget that it will be very difficult to ever balance it.

The debt situation is paralleled by our enormous balance-of-trade deficit. Foreign holders of our dollars have been recycling them into Treasury bills, but they're sick of it, so we have to keep our interest rates higher than they'd otherwise be in order to talk the Japanese and Taiwanese into owning more dollar assets. High interest rates can lead to recession, which cuts tax revenues and increases the debt even more.

It's a trap, all right, the unintended consequence of people trying to be nice—by giving away pensions and health care and unem-

ployment benefits and all that other good stuff people want. Perfectly decent countries like Canada, Belgium, and Ireland have also fallen into the trap and found how hard it is to work their way out.

By 1996, the administration and Congress were still struggling with the problem. It is clear that it would take draconian measures to balance the budget, and neither political party relishes risking the unpopularity of such measures. The restraints would, of course, have to be in place for years. It took decades to create the problem and it can't be fixed overnight. It's like someone who's a hundred pounds overweight. You can't lose that much weight without some suffering.

I worry that at some point we'll go back into an inflationary environment. It's so tempting to pay back debt in cheaper dollars. That's the only solution politicians can think of, because every other solution means they'd be diselected. Inflation is more palatable than unemployment. It is hard for any politician to resist the temptation to give out money from the Treasury without offsetting it by increasing taxes. That's the way you stay popular—and create an intolerable long-term situation.

In short, classical theory says that a massive federal deficit and a massive balance-of-trade deficit are going to work against the currency. With such a prospect, I want to own foreign as well as U.S. securities.

Don't keep all your assets in one currency.

The second argument in favor of diversifying into foreign markets is that in many countries where U.S. companies do business they are always going to be perceived as, and treated as, outsiders. Out-of-town money is welcome, but the locals take a delight in

making quick profits off newcomers, whether they are called *gaijin,* *gweilos, goyim,* or *gringos.* Our *emptor*s had better *caveat.* The local man will be given the advantage, especially by the native bureaucracy. There is a common tendency to take care of your own and freeze out foreigners, whether by legal or illegal means. Exchange controls, special regulations, all sorts of ways are devised to hamper the foreigner.

Locals always have an edge.

We've all read stories about how difficult it is for a U.S. company to do well in Japan. I know what's happened in my own industry. U.S. mutual fund companies—Fidelity and several others of the giants—have been trying to market a product in Europe and the Far East for years and have found it very difficult, because each of these countries has its own financial institutions and doesn't relish the idea of competitors from outside. So they've found eleven open and fourteen devious ways to prevent this competition from occurring.

Eventually all this will probably change. The trend is to the one world economy we all hear and read about. But it is going to be frustratingly slow in coming.

There's a third reason that sticking to U.S. multinationals isn't the same as directly investing abroad: some foreign industries simply don't have counterparts in the United States. For instance, in Singapore you can invest in shipyard stocks. There aren't any shipyard stocks in the U.S. In Britain you can buy an airport management company. There's no such thing here. Many of these stocks are very good investments.

Oh, yes, there's one more reason, at least for people in my line of work: the travel is terrific.

A Proven Path

In the ten years or so that I've been a serious investor in foreign stocks, I've followed the same philosophy and approach that shape my domestic-stock portfolios. I want the same above-average growth at a reasonable price, with the growth story supported by a long-term theme. Growth is best assured, offshore as on, by domination of a niche. I look for companies like Modern Photo Film, whose niche is filled by its exclusive license to make and sell Fuji film and cameras in Indonesia. And I have concentrated on small companies, though if you want to invest in some emerging markets, you are forced to choose from the few large companies that constitute the public market.

One of the great attractions of foreign stocks is that investing in small companies overseas now is like doing it here twenty-five years ago. I used to play a game on the brokers who came to our offices. I would hand the visitor our latest quarterly report and ask him to identify what businesses the companies in the portfolio were in. If he could recognize half of the names, I considered him well informed. Today the percentage recognized would be far higher. It's tough to find small companies in the U.S. that aren't followed to some degree by at least a regional firm, and the companies themselves are now accustomed to media releases and conference calls. Everyone hears any news within seconds, so it is extremely difficult to gain an information edge. But in many countries abroad the idea of telling investors anything is a new idea.

But once foreigners do start talking, they are often more open and candid than American corporate executives. The American is acutely aware of the implications of anything he says. Will he be disclosing something the SEC will say is inside information that he should have broadcast to the whole world? Might candid statements hurt his stock and, thereby, his personal net worth, much of which is tied up in stock options? The overseas manager is considerably less aware of regulators and stock prices, and he probably doesn't have options. He hasn't become skilled in double-talk. You can really learn what's going on.

Research coverage is still spotty enough that most overseas markets are far less efficient than our own. In 1989 my wife, Leah, found a small German software company, SAP AG, that we thought unusually cheap, mainly because German investors didn't understand it. The software business was too new for them to evaluate. Anyway, it was a growth stock, and German investors want asset-rich companies. Our German contacts assured us no one in Germany would buy SAP because it had no hard assets. They labeled it an "American" stock and more or less ignored it.

Investing in small companies overseas now is like investing in them in this country twenty five years ago.

We took a fairly large position in the stock and it did well enough. In time, Leah learned that earnings for the current year were probably going to be lower than German researchers were forecasting, so she sold the position. A whole month later, a Wall Street analyst called on the company and got the word on the earnings shortfall. A profits warning was issued and the stock promptly fell. In the United States a major earnings disappointment would have been discovered and passed through the entire investment community in hours, not a month. The stock fell far enough that she bought it back.

Then the company was discovered. It was the subject of a feature article in *Fortune* in September 1995, and it's now listed on the DAX, the German equivalent of the New York Stock Exchange. SAP has turned out to be one of the world's great integrated software companies. The stock became too popular, and we sold again. All told, we made about $100 million on SAP.

One can, in short, still turn up businesses abroad that others know little about—businesses growing at very fast rates. This is especially true in small-company stocks. For several years at least, I see enormous potential.

Risk Capital and National Cultures

One interesting anomaly deserves attention, however. By any standard, the U.S. economy is very mature. Yet we have some of the world's fastest-growing companies. With an occasional exception like SAP, companies like Wal-Mart and Sun Microsystems simply don't exist in Germany, for example. And I think our freewheeling culture is the reason. A whole industry exists to supply venture capital to people with an attractive idea. It's very respectable here to leave your job as an engineer at General Electric and start your own company, and you will get support. People will lend you money. People will do business with you. Perhaps more crucially, if you fail, it's no big deal. You can go back and get a job as an engineer, maybe even your old job at GE. In Germany, if you start a business and fail, you'll be known as a bankrupt and be ostracized. There is a social stigma attached to that particular kind of failure. You're made to feel as though you've dishonored your name for generations.

In Japan, the rate of formation of new companies is impressive, and despite the long cultural history that stresses the importance of saving face, there isn't the same sense of disgrace associated with entrepreneurial failures. But it's hard for new companies to become important companies, to poke their way up through the very tight, interlocking structure of Japanese business, especially if the entrepreneurs don't have the right connections with the ruling clique. In Japan you have a strong corporate culture but no shareholder culture. Everything that is done is designed for the benefit of the company. Concern for shareholders isn't valued very highly.

In the rest of the Far East, including China, you do have a great many entrepreneurs and start-up businesses, mostly family businesses. The question then is how many of these family-oriented businesses, many of them growing very rapidly, are going to have the ability to become true public companies, because one of these days they are going to run out of cousins. Can family cultures turn into institutionalized big businesses? It's a tough transition.

Overseas Themes

Themes may be even more important when investing in foreign markets than in our own, because it's vital abroad to have a long-term reason to hold a stock. Maybe because I'm a Chicagoan, familiar with how the Board of Trade and Mercantile Exchange operate, I've learned that you really can't outtrade the locals. They're pretty smart. If you want to day-trade soybeans in the United States, you'd better get in the pit and become one of the boys. In many foreign markets, too, you are up against strong trading mentalities. These fellows really like to roll the dice, and since inside trading is permissible and rife, the dice can be loaded. In Hong Kong and Thailand, as strong examples, the turnover is very high and stories are everywhere. If you, as an outsider, try to trade on stories, you are going to end up two weeks behind.

So the secret is to become a long-term investor, to adopt a different time scale from the one most of the locals go by. Then their edge washes out over time. The locals are just interested in running a stock up 25 percent and selling it. If you can be in for the long haul—sometimes buying the stocks the nationals are dumping—

and just sit with those stocks, you can realize the high growth available in these countries without being nailed by all the stories.

Also, with small-cap stocks, liquidity is a considerable problem in many of these markets. When you want to sell, the local brokers just giggle at you. So again, you need a long-term reason to hold on.

Sometimes you do get fed up with the smaller, developing markets—their illiquidity and volatility, the insiders' edge, the struggle to find out what's really going on. You have to remind yourself that with countries growing at 6 to 10 percent and companies growing at 25 to 30 percent, it's worth putting up with such inconveniences.

When investing abroad, you need a long-term reason for holding a stock, because you can't outtrade the locals.

One theme, discussed in an earlier chapter, stems from just such numbers. If the GNP growth rate in many countries is 6 to 10 percent—compared to 2 to 3 percent in the United States—then consumer disposable income is growing at a weird number like 15 to 20 percent. And you can be sure, whether it's Malaysia or Chile or China, people are going to follow the path the United States took when it went from a poor country to a middle-class country to a rich country. I can't think of any place in the world that, as it gets richer, doesn't eat more meat and protein foods and less bread and rice. Everybody would like to have nicer clothing, a car, and a large air-conditioned house, and feel entitled to a pair of Reeboks and a meal at McDonald's once in a while. Investors have to find the companies that satisfy these desires.

Another theme, a very important one that was also discussed in an earlier chapter, is the creation of communications systems in so many parts of the developing world. We've owned telephone and cellular phone companies in Korea, the Philippines, Brazil, and Italy. China would offer a fantastic opportunity, but the government has forbidden any foreign ownership of telecommunications facilities.

I've also mentioned the ship repair industry in Singapore. The Singapore yards are the lowest-cost yards in the world, and merchant fleets universally are in dire need of upgrading.

Another theme is printing and publishing. Newspaper advertising—and profits—rise rapidly as more and more readers move into the middle class. We've owned newspaper stocks in Holland, Norway, Turkey, Malaysia, and Hong Kong.

Distribution systems in the developing world offer another area of concentration. In Taiwan we own President Enterprises, which runs 7-Eleven stores; in Mexico, we've invested in Nadro, a pharmaceutical wholesaler.

Tigers Unleashed

China constitutes a theme unto itself. I believe the country today is in a position very like that of Japan in the early 1950s. China is reviving from the anarchy of its Communist rule the way Japan had to emerge from the devastation of World War II, and China can be equally successful, for its people are just as intelligent and hardworking. The Japanese market advanced more than three hundred–fold in the years following 1950. That miracle can be reenacted. At present most China investments are made through Hong Kong companies, but to some degree, all Southeast Asia is a China play. Direct investments will follow.

China is not going to be easy, however. When an investor first hears about China, it sounds like heaven. It has no lawyers and no accountants. But what you realize after a while is that China needs lawyers and accountants, because it needs honest books and written agreements and established, stable laws. You don't have them in China yet.

The Japanese market advanced more than three hundred-fold after 1950. That miracle can be reenacted in China.

But law and accountancy are coming. Country after country has seen the advantages of moving toward free markets, less government intervention, and lower taxes. These things work. They've worked in China, with particularly spectacular results, in the Special Economic Zones in the south. It would be very hard now to reverse the process and go back to a government-monopoly economy, because people have enjoyed upgrading from a bicycle to a motorcycle, from a radio to a color TV. What's more, the consumer revolution will lead to a political evolution toward a greater measure of democracy in China.

China Roused

Napoleon said, "Let China sleep, for when it wakes, it will shake the world." China went to sleep in the early fifteenth century. Back then its technology, culture, and government were far ahead of those of European, Indian, or Ottoman civilizations. But the Ming emperors cut off all contact with the West and sank back into complacent isolation. That was not a good long-run plan.

In the seventeenth century the country was overrun by Mongol armies, even though Mongol military technology was still based on cavalry armed with bows and arrows. China saw its Siberian dependencies stripped by Russia and control of its coastline lost to British and French naval power. By the late nineteenth century China was helpless, with its internal affairs confused by rebellions and banditry, and its borders under constant erosion by Russian, English, French, German, and Japanese imperialists.

Much of the twentieth century has brought nothing but more woe to China. After the Communists finally seized power, in 1949, they utterly failed to build a modern industrial nation. Mao's Great Leap Forward pushed the country backward. Then the Cultural Revolution cost China at least a decade of stagnation. China was an impoverished wreck, while Japan, Hong Kong, Singapore, and Taiwan prospered. China and Taiwan were about equally poor in 1949. By 1978 Taiwanese incomes approached European levels, while China was still mired in poverty.

After Mao died in 1976, China finally began to discard Communist ideology and work on economic growth—which proved remarkably rapid once the politicians were out of the way. Economic growth for countries is rather like cross-country skiing: the first one in line has to break the trail, which is hard work, but those coming after expend less energy if they just stay in the track. The economy of the most populous country on earth is now growing at a 9 percent annual clip, the rate at which Japan and Taiwan performed 25 years ago. Southern

China, now the hinterland of Hong Kong, has been expanding at 12 to 15 percent per year, with other coastal provinces close behind and the inland provinces, too, emerging from slumber. China is now awake, and we must face the consequences of this awakening.

The stock market potential is sensational. Japan is a precursor of what could happen. In 1950, Japan was in terrible shape, with the market at 100. Then Japanese growth took off. By 1969 the market hit 2400. In 1981 it had risen to 7500. By 1989, the Nikkei Index peaked at 38000 before the bubble burst (the index fell as low as 14000). The long-term results created a host of fantastically wealthy Japanese, especially since real estate prices were experiencing a similar bull market. The story was the same in Hong Kong, Taiwan, and other Asian countries.

It is already predicted that fairly early in the next century China's GNP will surpass not only Japan's but our own. China then will be as prosperous as Japan is today, but with ten times as many people.

If the preceding paragraph doesn't make you nervous, please reread it. Consider the trade issues that will arise. If you liked competing with Japan, you will love China. Estimate the air and water pollution that will occur. Graph out the consumption of oil, timber, fish, and other natural resources. Calculate the military potential of a country with 1.5 billion people and a modern industrial base. All of these are serious issues. There is little the United States can do about China's galloping growth except to persuade her that democracy and international cooperation are in her own best interest.

And *Japan*? Problems persist. Its economy is quite mature now, which means we can expect only moderate growth. But a political and social revolution is under way that will create some interesting investment opportunities. My theme for Japan is that it is moving from a producer society controlled by middle-aged men to a consumer society in which women will have a major role. I expect a swing away from exporting and capital goods companies toward companies involved in housing and retailing. So you try to guess who's going to be the Home Depot or Wal-Mart of Japan. So far we have not found a satisfactory answer.

Japan is moving from a producer society controlled by middle-aged men to a consumer society in which women will have a major role.

India could be very exciting. The theme here is the same as for China—the reform of a socialist economy. India fits the Promethean metaphor of a giant in chains. The chains were the bureaucratic rules that governed every aspect of corporate activity. Finally some ministers came into government who said if businesses are run by competent people, they'll do sensible things. If they don't, the businessmen will fail and be replaced by others who will do sensible things. Therefore, we can take away a bunch of rules. It's worked. India's been moving along at about a 6 percent growth rate, up from its historic rate of about 3 percent.

Korea is a special situation. It wasn't opened to foreigners until 1992, and foreigners can still own only 10 percent of a company's outstanding shares (and in some cases foreign ownership is forbidden altogether). Since the quality, liquid stocks quickly reached the 10 percent limit, the only way you can buy these shares is from another foreigner, and you must pay a premium over local prices. Premiums have been as high as 60 percent. We've owned a few stocks we felt were cheap even with the premium, but this is another instance where the individual investor would be in over his head.

Other Asian countries have become boom centers, of course, and *Latin America* revived magnificently once governments relaxed their strangleholds on economies. *Eastern Europe* has some promising equity markets, though liquidity is shallow. There's little foreign investment in *Africa* outside South Africa, except by the World Bank and International Monetary Fund, but exchanges are being built.

And then there is *Russia*. It is still at the venture capital stage: the money being invested is from corporate and private venture funds. There's no equity market to speak of. The legal structures don't exist yet. Tax rates and regulations change frequently and unpredictably. Conflicts between Moscow and the provincial and local governments are daily fare.

We're all familiar with Russia's ugly problems—inflation and unemployment, separatist struggles, corruption, organized crime and simple theft, the rise of neo-Communist and neofascist parties—and the predictions of chaos, civil war, and the ascension of a new strongman. However, we don't see headlines about food riots; people are at least being fed. Thousands of Russians are getting rich (by various means), and a middle class will emerge. I was impressed by the analysis in Daniel Yergin and Thane Gustafson's 1993 book, *Russia 2010 and What It Means for the World.* The authors are smart enough not to make a single forecast. They develop various possible political scenarios: democracy may triumph or authoritarian rule may return. But by 2010 the economy, they believe, will prove a success story, which means it may yet be a place where ordinary investors can make some money.

Spread Your Bets

At Acorn our main emphasis is on picking companies rather than countries, but it's important to make some top-down judgments as well. You don't want much exposure in unstable countries. Too many people assume their money will be safe in places where they wouldn't drink the water. In assessing how comfortable we feel about investing in a country, we consider the usual factors of political risk, inflation and interest rates, balance of payments, and the like. We want to feel the country is on the right track.

Too many people assume their money will be safe in countries where they wouldn't drink the water.

And because you can't eliminate all risk and still invest overseas, we diversify. We always maintain a certain amount of skepticism about our opinions in any case, whether we're investing domestically or abroad. We know we are fallible. So diversification is part of our faith. Acorn International owns stocks in forty countries, and Acorn itself, which has about a quarter of its portfolio in non-U.S. stocks, nearly as many. Obviously, with that many countries, some are classified as emerging markets, where diversification is particularly vital.

Companies often have to be judged differently in different countries. In Japan, for example, companies are mostly run by corporate types; faceless management is in charge. Elsewhere in Asia the businesses are run by families, and you have to find out whether or not the family has a reputation for integrity.

Though the big Wall Street houses are constantly adding to their research coverage of non-U.S. companies, I've tried as much as possible to work with local brokers. The local broker is simply closer to the company, so we think we get better information on a more timely basis. Also, we are important to that broker. If we relied on Merrill Lynch's research on a European company, for example, we would expect Merrill to call Fidelity or T. Rowe Price or some other more important client before it called us with an interesting bit of news.

It's Tough on Your Own

You, as an individual investor, can't build a network of brokers around the globe. You'd have to rely on Merrill Lynch.

It's getting easier to be a direct investor overseas, as U.S. brokerage firms build expertise and enter into alliances with overseas brokers, but there are still many difficulties in tracking companies, assessing economies, worrying about currencies, and dealing with local regulations, accounting differences, and indifference to stock manipulations. Individual investors couldn't replicate a mutual fund's portfolio for custodial reasons alone: you couldn't find a U.S. broker that would hold some of the stocks that funds own. Any seasoned international investor can recite a bundle of horror stories and tell you how long it took him or her to learn the ropes.

But the chief argument for relying on mutual funds is that professionals traversing the globe to develop corporate and analyst relationships are able to dig up investments that a private investor couldn't hope to find. Acorn has owned a casino operator in Malaysia, a newspaper in the Netherlands, a ceramic tile maker in Mexico, a cable TV operator in Switzerland, a multiplex movie theater owner in Australia, a temporary-help company in France, a discount retailer in Japan, a window frame manufacturer in Germany, a bicycle maker in China, a cruise line in Italy, a cellular phone company in England, and an investment trust that invests in Brazil.

How are you, on your own, going to match the diverse package of opportunities a mutual fund can uncover?

Mutual funds traversing the globe to build corporate and broker relationships can dig up investments that a private investor could never hope to find.

The Rewards

The payoff for all this globe-trotting in search of the overlooked and misperceived? If the long-term return from U.S. stocks is about 10 percent annually and you hope to find a manager who can earn you better than that—12 to 15 percent on average is a reasonable goal—I'd say you can, without being overly aggressive, hope for 17 or 18 percent a year, on average, with your foreign stocks over time. That would be a very handsome return indeed.

A combination of U.S. and non-U.S. stocks produces a higher return *with less risk* than a 100 percent U.S. portfolio.

What's more, a recent study, conducted by Morgan Stanley Capital International, showed that a combination of U.S. and non-U.S. stocks produced a higher return *with less risk* (the proverbial free lunch may be attainable after all) than a 100 percent U.S. portfolio. The allocation that promises the highest return with least risk would be a 60 percent U.S. and 40 percent non-U.S. combination. If you went to 80 percent non-U.S. stocks, your risk would rise to about the same level as if you had a 100 percent U.S. portfolio—but your return would also rise, by a couple of percentage points. The study covered the period from 1985 through 1993, so it included both the 1987 market quake felt around the world and the Gulf War, which also sent all markets tumbling. The percentages could change with different time frames, but the overall results will be similar.

The issue really isn't whether or not you should invest in foreign stocks. The issue is whether or not you should be in stocks altogether. If you are in pain when a stock or stock mutual fund drops 5 percent, the answer is negative. But if you *are* a stock investor, you should be country-blind.

12

▟▟▟▟▟▟▟▟▟▟▟▟▟▟▟▟▟▟▟▟▟▟▟

PARTING REMINDERS

There are basic laws that control the investing universe, just as Newton's laws control the physical universe. I didn't discover them, but I have tested them in portfolio laboratories for many years and can verify their power. They have properties that attract wealth.

LAW I: Compound Interest

Like all these laws, this is a very simple one. It says that if you have patience, your money pile can get very big.

You've seen the charts. Seven percent bonds will double your money in ten years if you reinvest the interest at the same rate. So even bonds can make you rich, given a few decades. Stocks treat you better, of course. The sooner you start, the more compounding can do for you. If, beginning at the age of twenty, you sock away just $100 a month in stocks, and your portfolio compounds at 10 percent, which is what stocks have provided historically, you will be a millionaire when you retire at sixty-five. Save and invest, and save and invest some more, and you will be able to live very nicely indeed without having had to worry a lot about what the market's up to this week or whether or not you chose the mutual fund that will be ranked number one in the next issue of *Money*.

But try telling that to someone who's twenty. Who cares about retirement when there's a great pair of speakers on sale at Circuit City? But talk to someone who's sixty-five and you are likely to hear, "If only I had paid attention years ago."

LAW II: Reversion to the Mean

Growth rates eventually go back to their long-term average. Trees don't grow to the sky, for reasons already explained. Reversion to the mean eventually provides the end to the inconsistencies of compound interest. Stock averages can soar at 20 percent for a while, but eventually the long-term return will be around 10 percent. This law, says economist Peter Bernstein in his fascinating book *Against the Gods*, "explains why pride goeth before a fall and why clouds tend to have silver linings." It predicts that great companies won't stay great companies forever. The great ones of thirty years ago are no longer on the top of the list. Eventually, even Microsoft will start to look like any other company.

Reversion to the mean is also why we have market cycles. In the real world, the growth rates are going to be 1 to 4 percent, the rate at which populations can grow, gross national products can grow, real corporate profits can grow. There are certain small regions of the world that are going to do better or worse than that for limited periods, but over the long sweep of time they, too, must reflect the same growth rate.

That's the pace of the real world, but the pricing of financial assets is quite a different matter. A tunnel under the English Channel is difficult, dangerous, and slow to construct. But the price of the stock of the company that owns the tunnel is very easy to change. It can go up or down 20 percent in a week. Financial prices move very rapidly, while changes in the real world tend to be sticky.

But eventually, the real world and the financial world have to mesh, because the value of the stock market—that is, the valuations of businesses—can't grow at a rate that is very much different from that of everything else. Stocks are part of society, of the real world. That's why studies of the long-term returns of the market come out with the figure of 9 to 10 percent—roughly 6 percent reflecting a growth in corporate net worth and 3 to 4 percent, dividends paid to shareholders. The 6 percent growth in corporate assets is related to the growth of the corporate sector generally and therefore a not implausible number.

For a time the stock market can appreciate considerably more than 6 percent a year (forgetting dividends), but it must, in accord with the law of reversion to the mean, get back to where it's providing a long-term return, before dividends, of 6 percent. Therefore, you have to have market cycles. If the market has been above the trend line for a spell, something is going to drag it back down below the trend line.

Some have said that with all the money pouring into stock mutual funds, especially with a regularity assured by 401(k) and other self-directed retirement plans—which, as you remember, generated one of my current investment themes—the market will be continuously buoyed. Corrections can only be shallow. The market's climb upward will be smoother and inexorable. Don't believe it.

Mutual fund managers may seem to control the market today, the way the trust departments did in my first years in this business, but in fact they don't control anything. They are merely purchasing agents. You must compare us with someone hired to water the garden. That person can decide whether to spray the roses first or the azaleas first, but his basic job is to stand there and spray. If you give mutual funds money to buy stocks, they'll buy stocks. Oh, some money can be kept in cash, and it seems to be big news if mutual fund cash levels go from 6 percent to 8 percent, but that's really of no long-term importance. All of the money that comes in gets invested. Any intermediary—be it mutual funds or trust departments—can appear to be supporting prices, but eventually the market has to kick back toward the long-term average.

If the system convinces everyone that it has evolved into an ever-upward path, it means only that more distortion is being stored up before the reversion comes. The more sophisticated the system that maintains the distortion, the bigger the smash ahead. You might well find out that what you're going to end up with is the mother of all bear markets. It has to happen. It happened in Japan. It will happen here after the distortion builds to an untenable level. We have to get back to the average.

This is what the market timers try to predict, of course, because it is easy to say the market has gone too far one way or the other. Trouble is, it is very hard to say *when* the correction will occur. It's like earthquakes: the energy has to be released, but we can't predict when.

Earthquakes are an apt metaphor here. Earthquakes are the end result of two tectonic plates moving relative to each other, an enormously energy-creating event. As long as the plates stick together, life is quite peaceful and pleasant. But the energy in that fault continuously builds and builds. When the plates eventually release that energy, we have an earthquake. It is quite easy to predict how much energy is going to be released in the next century by the San Andreas Fault, but we cannot predict just where along the fault that energy release will occur, or on what day it will happen.

In the same way, you can see that as the market goes up and up, the energy stored in it is going to have to be released and an explosion occur that will bring the market back down toward its long-term level of return. But whether that's going to happen tomorrow or next year is not so easily found out. Most people who have tried to predict the hour haven't done very well at it.

LAW III: Options Have Value

I don't mean the options traded on the Chicago Board of Exchange or other exchanges. I mean looking at securities in terms of their option component.

The simplest example is probably an oil company. It will have two components of value. One is the value of existing properties, which generate cash flows. You can calculate the present value of those cash flows, which will decline as the producing wells give out. The other component of value of an oil stock is the call option you have on the chance that the company will find a major new field. That bit of luck would create new value for stockholders.

The theoretical worth of the company is the sum of the value of existing production and the call option. It is very pleasant to find a stock that can be bought for the value of existing properties, so that the exploration option is free. It is even pleasanter if you can find a stock whose existing properties can be bought for *less* than the value of their present and future cash flows, again getting a free lottery ticket on some new product or other upside potential. An option is basically just that—a lottery ticket—and there's no sense in refusing a lottery ticket if you don't have to pay for it.

Sometimes you are asked to pay a great deal for those options; biotech stocks are a prime example. In a highly speculative market, people pay a great deal of money for the privilege of a claim on future success.

Usually, stocks have some kind of discernible option attached, but in other cases it is negligible, uninteresting, or at least very hard to find. And there are cases where the option seems to be more of a put option than a call option; the option component has a negative value. Tobacco stocks are an example. The cash flow from the cigarette business is stable and valuable, but there is a risk that regulatory or legal action will wreck the business. The stock price can be calculated as the value of the cash flow minus a put option.

Or both a call and a put option may be present. A drug company may be working on a new product that could turn into a huge success or trigger a product lawsuit that results in an enormous drain on earnings.

I have found it very helpful to analyze companies this way—to look at the stock world as a collection of measurable values with options attached.

LAW IV: Many Financial Offerings Are Nothing More than Ponzi Schemes

In a Ponzi scheme, money is taken from new suckers and divided among the early contributors. A chain letter is a kind of Ponzi scheme. As the number of participants in a scheme expands, you need new money at a rapidly increasing rate to keep it going, and at some point not enough new dupes can be found, and the whole thing collapses. It happened to Ponzi. It happened to Mike Milken and his firm, Drexel Burnham Lambert: they financed junk bonds by getting people who bought the last issue to put up money for the next one. It's happening to governments and their social security systems, as we examined in Chapter 6.

The real estate market was a Ponzi scheme that lasted a very long time. Serious studies declared, in essence, "Hey, everybody, real estate always has high returns and low volatility," and for many years it did, because so many people were pumping money into it, trading properties with one another for ever-increasing prices. And new people were continually being sucked in. It worked to the point where the real estate business grew so big that not enough new money could be dragged in from the outside to sustain the kited prices. In 1996 the U.S. real estate market was still recovering from its crash of a decade earlier. The Japanese real estate market, whose bubble burst in 1989, is still on its back.

You can argue that the whole stock market is a Ponzi scheme.

Stocks can keep selling at prices that are higher than their fundamental value as long as new suckers come along and put their money in. It certainly explains what happened to the Japanese stock market.

The investor should never have Law IV far from his mind.

LAW V: Every Bad Idea Starts from a Good Idea

We all know this from our own experience. We go to a party and have a glass of champagne. Good idea. We feel better, more relaxed. The party is now more interesting, the toasts more lively, the girls prettier, the dancing more fun. So we have a second glass of champagne. Another good idea. The jokes now have gone from humorous to hilarious, the people you're meeting are the most interesting and glamorous you've ever known, and the dancing is wild and you've never been better at it. But after the third glass, and the fourth . . . well, what started as a good idea turns into a very bad idea, with your head already beginning to pound from a headache you know will terminate in a humdinger of a hangover.

It happens all the time in the stock market. As I codify this law in mid-1996, technology stocks have been the rage for a long time, albeit with some periods of "consolidation." The boom started with a very good idea. American technology leads the world. Personal computers and the software to run them and other electronic and communications devices have become inexpensive and relatively easy to use, and we all buy them. Companies like Microsoft, Motorola, Intel are well-run—indeed, fabulous—companies. All this is correct. A great investment idea. The people who were in early have made a lot of money.

But as the party lengthens, the stocks get taken over by people who don't particularly understand what's happening; they are just playing a trend. And new companies are invented to meet their demands. The securities industry, you know, is not a service industry.

It is a manufacturing industry. If you want a stock, Wall Street will make it for you. Any business, any kind you want. Recently, the Internet being the rage, the investment bankers have worked overtime creating a stream of IPOs to meet the demand. And people love them, to judge by their P/Es, some of which have soared into the triple-digit stratosphere.

Remember back in the early eighties when the hard disk drive for computers was invented? It was an important, crucial invention, and investors were eager to be part of this technology. More than seventy disk drive companies were formed and their stocks were sold to the public. Each company had to get 20 percent of the market share to survive. For some reason, they didn't all do it.

Anything can get overdone. In the financial world, things get taken to extremes all the time, like the tulip scandal of 1637. That started with a good idea. The tulip was a terrific invention. The flower had not previously been seen in Europe, and it was a great hit, and new varieties and colors increased its popularity. There was nothing wrong with the idea. But after a few years people started selling tulip bulbs for hundreds of thousands of dollars apiece, if they were of a rare variety, and a good idea went to speculative madness.

The tulip was a good idea, disk drives were a good idea, the Internet is a good idea. They have to be good ideas or they would not become widely popular. Come up with a concept that's patently silly or harmful and people won't want it. If you open a resort whose main attraction is rock climbing up two-hundred-foot vertical faces, you can't expect it to be popular with those who have reached the age of reason. Only a small part of the population is that fond of strains and sprains. But if you start a business that sends a large steamship cruising around the middle of the ocean while the people on board get to eat and drink and dance and party, you have turned up a quite good idea. People like to do those things.

But remember, there can be too much of even a good thing.

GO FORTH AND PROSPER

Those are five golden rules for you. They all really do meld together, along with the other advice I've offered, which they should, if one has a consistent point of view about investing. Mine hasn't changed much from my early days in money management. It has only been reinforced, and refined a bit, by years of experience.

Maintain independence of thought and a healthy degree of skepticism, so you won't be drawn into the herd. Don't overpay, no matter how much you like a company. Invest in themes that will give a company a long-term franchise. Invest downstream from technology. Think and invest globally. Find stocks to own, not trade.

It's not all that complicated. Common sense and patience make a successful investor.

ACKNOWLEDGMENTS

My profound thanks to those who have made contributions to the substance and realization of this book:

Irving B. Harris, chairman of the Acorn Investment Trust, my mentor for nearly forty years;

The partners of Wanger Asset Management, a team of brilliant professionals: Chuck McQuaid, Terry Hogan, Marcel Houtzager, Rob Mohn, and Leah Zell;

Kathy Tucker, my assistant, for her long hours on this project; Mac Nelson and Jason Zweig, for their invaluable editing of the manuscript;

Everett Mattlin, my coauthor, who provided the discipline to get this book done;

Fred Hills, my editor at Simon & Schuster, for his patience, guidance, and professional skills in making this book accessible to a general readership;

My mother, Mary Jane Slepyan, and my five marvelous children, Eric, Leonard, Debra, Jenny, and Elise.

And finally, I want to thank Harry Bagal, manager of the Lane Bryant mail-order facility in Indianapolis, for firing me in 1960, thus freeing me to obtain a job as a security analyst in Chicago.

INDEX

INDEX